CW00684060

# Official

# SQA
## Past Papers
### WITH ANSWERS

# Higher
# French

## 2010–2014

| | |
|---|---|
| Hodder Gibson Study Skills Advice – General | – page 3 |
| Hodder Gibson Study Skills Advice – Higher French | – page 5 |
| **2010 EXAM** | – page 7 |
| Reading and Directed Writing – Listening Transcript – Listening/Writing | |
| **2011 EXAM** | – page 21 |
| Reading and Directed Writing – Listening Transcript – Listening/Writing | |
| **2012 EXAM** | – page 35 |
| Reading and Directed Writing – Listening Transcript – Listening/Writing | |
| **2013 EXAM** | – page 49 |
| Reading and Directed Writing – Listening Transcript – Listening/Writing | |
| **2014 EXAM** | – page 63 |
| **ANSWER SECTION** | – page 77 |

**HODDER GIBSON**
AN HACHETTE UK COMPANY

Hodder Gibson is grateful to the copyright holders, as credited on the final page of the Question Section, for permission to use their material. Every effort has been made to trace the copyright holders and to obtain their permission for the use of copyright material. Hodder Gibson will be happy to receive information allowing us to rectify any error or omission in future editions.

Hachette UK's policy is to use papers that are natural, renewable and recyclable products and made from wood grown in sustainable forests. The logging and manufacturing processes are expected to conform to the environmental regulations of the country of origin.

Orders: please contact Bookpoint Ltd, 130 Park Drive, Abingdon, Oxon OX14 4SE. Telephone: (44) 01235 827720. Fax: (44) 01235 400454.

Lines are open 9.00–5.00, Monday to Saturday, with a 24-hour message answering service. Visit our website at www.hoddereducation.co.uk. Hodder Gibson can be contacted direct on: Tel: 0141 848 1609; Fax: 0141 889 6315; email: hoddergibson@hodder.co.uk

This collection first published in 2014 by

Hodder Gibson, an imprint of Hodder Education,

An Hachette UK Company

2a Christie Street

Paisley PA1 1NB

{BrightRED  Hodder Gibson is grateful to Bright Red Publishing Ltd for collaborative work in preparation of this book and all SQA Past Paper, National 5 and Higher for CfE Model Paper titles 2014.

Typeset by PDQ Digital Media Solutions Ltd, Bungay, Suffolk NR35 1BY

Printed in the UK

A catalogue record for this title is available from the British Library

ISBN 978-1-4718-3681-7

3 2 1

2015 2014

# Introduction

## Study Skills – what you need to know to pass exams!

### Pause for thought

Many students might skip quickly through a page like this. After all, we all know how to revise. Do you really though?

### Think about this:

"IF YOU ALWAYS DO WHAT YOU ALWAYS DO, YOU WILL ALWAYS GET WHAT YOU HAVE ALWAYS GOT."

Do you like the grades you get? Do you want to do better? If you get full marks in your assessment, then that's great! Change nothing! This section is just to help you get that little bit better than you already are.

There are two main parts to the advice on offer here. The first part highlights fairly obvious things but which are also very important. The second part makes suggestions about revision that you might not have thought about but which WILL help you.

### Part 1

DOH! It's so obvious but …

### Start revising in good time

Don't leave it until the last minute – this will make you panic.

Make a revision timetable that sets out work time AND play time.

### Sleep and eat!

Obvious really, and very helpful. Avoid arguments or stressful things too – even games that wind you up. You need to be fit, awake and focused!

### Know your place!

Make sure you know exactly **WHEN and WHERE** your exams are.

### Know your enemy!

**Make sure you know what to expect in the exam.**

How is the paper structured?

How much time is there for each question?

What types of question are involved?

Which topics seem to come up time and time again?

Which topics are your strongest and which are your weakest?

Are all topics compulsory or are there choices?

### Learn by DOING!

There is no substitute for past papers and practice papers – they are simply essential! Tackling this collection of papers and answers is exactly the right thing to be doing as your exams approach.

### Part 2

People learn in different ways. Some like low light, some bright. Some like early morning, some like evening / night. Some prefer warm, some prefer cold. But everyone uses their BRAIN and the brain works when it is active. Passive learning – sitting gazing at notes – is the most INEFFICIENT way to learn anything. Below you will find tips and ideas for making your revision more effective and maybe even more enjoyable. What follows gets your brain active, and active learning works!

### Activity 1 – Stop and review

#### Step 1

When you have done no more than 5 minutes of revision reading STOP!

#### Step 2

Write a heading in your own words which sums up the topic you have been revising.

#### Step 3

Write a summary of what you have revised in no more than two sentences. Don't fool yourself by saying, "I know it, but I cannot put it into words". That just means you don't know it well enough. If you cannot write your summary, revise that section again, knowing that you must write a summary at the end of it. Many of you will have notebooks full of blue/black ink writing. Many of the pages will not be especially attractive or memorable so try to liven them up a bit with colour as you are reviewing and rewriting. **This is a great memory aid, and memory is the most important thing.**

## Activity 2 — Use technology!

Why should everything be written down? Have you thought about "mental" maps, diagrams, cartoons and colour to help you learn? And rather than write down notes, why not record your revision material?

What about having a text message revision session with friends? Keep in touch with them to find out how and what they are revising and share ideas and questions.

Why not make a video diary where you tell the camera what you are doing, what you think you have learned and what you still have to do? No one has to see or hear it, but the process of having to organise your thoughts in a formal way to explain something is a very important learning practice.

Be sure to make use of electronic files. You could begin to summarise your class notes. Your typing might be slow, but it will get faster and the typed notes will be easier to read than the scribbles in your class notes. Try to add different fonts and colours to make your work stand out. You can easily Google relevant pictures, cartoons and diagrams which you can copy and paste to make your work more attractive and **MEMORABLE**.

## Activity 3 – This is it. Do this and you will know lots!

### Step 1

In this task you must be very honest with yourself! Find the SQA syllabus for your subject (www.sqa.org.uk). Look at how it is broken down into main topics called MANDATORY knowledge. That means stuff you MUST know.

### Step 2

BEFORE you do ANY revision on this topic, write a list of everything that you already know about the subject. It might be quite a long list but you only need to write it once. It shows you all the information that is already in your long-term memory so you know what parts you do not need to revise!

### Step 3

Pick a chapter or section from your book or revision notes. Choose a fairly large section or a whole chapter to get the most out of this activity.

With a buddy, use Skype, Facetime, Twitter or any other communication you have, to play the game "If this is the answer, what is the question?". For example, if you are revising Geography and the answer you provide is "meander", your buddy would have to make up a question like "What is the word that describes a feature of a river where it flows slowly and bends often from side to side?".

Make up 10 "answers" based on the content of the chapter or section you are using. Give this to your buddy to solve while you solve theirs.

### Step 4

Construct a wordsearch of at least 10 X 10 squares. You can make it as big as you like but keep it realistic. Work together with a group of friends. Many apps allow you to make wordsearch puzzles online. The words and phrases can go in any direction and phrases can be split. Your puzzle must only contain facts linked to the topic you are revising. Your task is to find 10 bits of information to hide in your puzzle, but you must not repeat information that you used in Step 3. DO NOT show where the words are. Fill up empty squares with random letters. Remember to keep a note of where your answers are hidden but do not show your friends. When you have a complete puzzle, exchange it with a friend to solve each other's puzzle.

### Step 5

Now make up 10 questions (not "answers" this time) based on the same chapter used in the previous two tasks. Again, you must find NEW information that you have not yet used. Now it's getting hard to find that new information! Again, give your questions to a friend to answer.

### Step 6

As you have been doing the puzzles, your brain has been actively searching for new information. Now write a NEW LIST that contains only the new information you have discovered when doing the puzzles. Your new list is the one to look at repeatedly for short bursts over the next few days. Try to remember more and more of it without looking at it. After a few days, you should be able to add words from your second list to your first list as you increase the information in your long-term memory.

## FINALLY! Be inspired...

Make a list of different revision ideas and beside each one write **THINGS I HAVE** tried, **THINGS I WILL** try and **THINGS I MIGHT** try. Don't be scared of trying something new.

And remember – "FAIL TO PREPARE AND PREPARE TO FAIL!"

# Higher French

## The course

The Higher qualification in French develops students' abilities in the four language skills of Speaking, Listening, Reading and Writing. The content of the course is drawn from three prescribed themes: *Lifestyles, Education and Work*, and *the Wider World*, which subdivide into six topic areas. These are the topics you will have studied in depth and these are the same topics which the examiners will use to test you in the final examination. When speaking, listening, reading and writing on these topics at Higher level, **the content** will deal with more complex issues, ideas and a range of opinions. **The language** you have to understand and use in French will also be more complex and will contain a greater range and variety of vocabulary, verb tenses and grammatical structures.

### How the course is graded

The grade you are finally awarded for Higher French depends on three elements:

- the internal assessments you do in school or college (the "NABs") – these don't count towards the final grade, but you must have passed them before you can achieve a final grade

- your Speaking assessment – this is recorded and assessed by your teacher at the end of March and the mark is then submitted to SQA and counts for 25% of your final grade

- the two external assessments which you sit in May and which test Reading/Translation (30% of your final grade), Listening (20% of your final grade) and Writing (25% of your final grade). Making sure you are well prepared to give your best performance in these two external assessments is what this book is all about! So bon travail et bonne chance!

## The exam

The following information and advice is intended to help you plan and prepare for the external examination at Higher level. It is based on advice given by the Principal Examiner as to how candidates can best approach the different elements of the exam in order to achieve the best possible performance. **Tips** are presented firstly on how best to approach the papers which test comprehension (Paper 1: Reading and Translation, and Paper 2: Listening) and secondly the papers which test Writing (Paper 1: Directed Writing, and Paper 2: Writing Personal Opinion). Try reading the hints and tips and then put them into practice by completing the relevant past paper!

### Tips for Reading

1. **BEFORE** trying to work out the meaning of the text, always read the introduction to the passage and the questions. These are in English and give important information as to what the different parts of the passage are about and also the type of information you need to find in order to answer the questions.

2. **Keep your use of the dictionary to a minimum. You won't have time to look up every word and the dictionary is not a substitute for learning key vocabulary!** Target your revision of vocabulary on the most common words from the prescribed themes of *Lifestyles, Education and Work* and *the Wider World*. Try using your knowledge of English, French vocabulary and French grammar to work out the meaning of any words that you don't immediately understand. Does the word look like an English word e.g. **libérer** = to liberate/free? Does it look like a French word you know but is being used for a different grammatical purpose e.g. **rougir** = infinitive of **-ir** verb; (**rouge** = red (adjective) so **rougir = to become red/blush**). However, also look out for 'false friends' i.e. words which look like an English word but mean something else. Three of the most common ones are **la journée** (the day, not the journey which is **le voyage**), **la lecture** (reading) and **rester** (to remain or stay not to rest which is **se reposer**).

3. The number of marks available for each question will **guide** you as to how much detail and information to include in your answers! For each question, find the relevant information in the text and try to answer in clear and comprehensible English. Don't translate word for word from the passage or you will end up with nonsensical sentences in English.

### Tips for Translation

1. Only attempt the translation once you have answered what you can of the reading comprehension questions.

2. Be very accurate when working out the meaning of each of the five sections. Candidates often lose marks for being "**imprecise or inaccurate**" because of careless translation of words such as "**son/sa/ses**" (his/her), "**ce/cette/ces**" (this/these), pronouns such as "**on** (one/we) / **lui** (to him/her) / **leur** (to them)" or of verb tenses e.g. translating a conditional tense "**j'irais**" as the future "I will go" (**j'irai**) or the imperfect "I was going/used to go" (**j'allais**).

**3.** Having worked out exactly what each section means, then decide how best to translate this into English which is **accurate but not awkward**.

## Tips for Listening

**1.** As in the Reading exam, it is important to have revised vocabulary from the key prescribed themes and topics, such as opinions on school, home area, family relationships and healthy living. Also don't forget to revise numbers (times and prices), dates (days and months), weather expressions and seasons, as they should be easy to pick out from any listening text! Make sure that you pick up these easier points by recognising time phrases such as "**avant** (before)", "**après** (after)", "**depuis** (since/for)", "**il y a** (ago)", "**la semaine dernière** (last)", and "**l'été prochain** (next)". Many candidates lose marks because they are unable to retain sufficient details required to answer accurately the questions, often understanding part of the information but not giving sufficient details e.g. des sports **d'équipe** (**team** sports) / **moins de** devoirs (**less** homework) / gens **de mon âge** (people **my age**).

**2.** Before you hear the listening text for the first time, you will have two minutes to look at the question paper and this will give you an indication of what you are about to hear. Use this time in order to anticipate the sort of French you might expect to hear given the context! In particular, look at each question and see what sort of information you will need to find e.g. When? = time phrase / date etc. Where? = directions / preposition and place e.g. **en face de la poste**. Use the number of marks available as a guide as to how much information you will need to find.

**3.** Your answers don't need to be in sentences but they must be clear and comprehensible. Be sure to score out any earlier notes and don't leave alternative answers because if one is right and one is wrong, you will end up with no points!!

## Tips for Writing

**1.** To be at least "Satisfactory" your writing at Higher level "must convey meaning clearly", which means you must be able to handle common verbs accurately enough so that it is clear if the action is happening in the present, past or future. To gain a higher mark you will need to maintain a high level of grammatical accuracy and begin to write more complex sentences using a greater range of vocabulary and structures. What you must avoid is making "serious basic errors" and introducing "mother tongue interference" through thinking in English and misusing the dictionary.

**2.** **Paper 1 (b) Directed Writing (150–180 words).** The format of this test is predictable but the scenario will change from year to year, as will the wording of the 6 bullet points of information that you must include. The first two bullet points are very predictable and require you to set the scene by giving details of what the journey was like, where you stayed (use **loger** not **rester** for "to stay"), how many were in the group etc. The other bullet points are less predictable but are likely to focus on the purpose of your visit, what you did during your stay, what you thought of it and what future benefit you will get from it. Therefore you need to have a confident command of past tenses (imperfect and perfect) and future and conditional tenses.

**3.** **Paper 2 Listening/Writing (120–150 words).** This writing task is related to the topic of the listening and you must write a personal response based on a stimulus in French, which asks questions that you must use to structure the content of your response. What you write **must be relevant to these questions** so don't try to reproduce an entire pre-learned essay but try to select and re-combine material that you have learned and practised throughout the year. Remember that at Higher level you will have done writing tasks throughout the year in preparation for your speaking assessment and you will have lots of good ideas and phrases from them that you should seek to re-use in the exam. Only use the dictionary to check the accuracy (le/le/les) or spelling (accents) **NOT** to translate sentences from English to French!

## FINAL TIP

In all papers, but especially in the Writing papers, **make sure your handwriting is legible!**

# Good luck!

Remember that the rewards for passing Higher French are well worth it! Your pass will help you get the future you want for yourself. In the exam, be confident in your own ability. If you're not sure how to answer a question, trust your instincts and just give it a go anyway. Keep calm and don't panic! GOOD LUCK!

HODDER
GIBSON
LEARN MORE

[BLANK PAGE]

# X059/301

NATIONAL
QUALIFICATIONS
2010

TUESDAY, 18 MAY
9.00 AM – 10.40 AM

FRENCH
HIGHER
Reading and
Directed Writing

45 marks are allocated to this paper. The value attached to each question is shown after each question.

You should spend approximately one hour on Section I and 40 minutes on Section II.

You may use a French dictionary.

## SECTION I—READING

Read the whole article carefully and then answer **in English** the questions which follow it.

This passage tells us about how young people can get into financial difficulty.

### Les Jeunes et leur Argent

C'est avec la rentrée des classes que le déluge de publicité commence. Les étudiants ne seront jamais plus riches qu'à ce moment-là. Après un été de
5 travail payé, ils ont de l'argent à brûler. Argent que des entreprises de toutes sortes lorgnent[1] d'un oeil intéressé.

Les étudiants qui retournent au
10 collège ou à l'université se font bombarder de dépliants et de promesses. Pour le prix d'un téléphone portable, un service Internet ou une carte de crédit, paraît-il, leur
15 popularité et leur bonheur seront garantis. C'est la règle cardinale du marketing jeunesse – offrez-leur un beau petit cadeau super-cool: vidéos exclusives, musique gratuite . . . Et
20 cela vaut la peine: le marché étudiant est d'une grande importance pour les entreprises qui en font de gros profits.

Cette sorte de publicité s'applique partout, mais attire particulièrement
25 les jeunes. Les jeunes d'aujourd'hui contribuent peu aux dépenses familiales, avec le résultat que presque tout leur argent est utilisé pour financer leurs loisirs. Et ils ont
30 tendance à penser que le bonheur, c'est acheter, posséder toujours plus.

### Anita, Acheteuse Compulsive

Anita, par exemple, est étudiante de langues vivantes à la fac de Lille. Elle
35 rêve de voyager pour perfectionner ses langues mais elle ne peut rien faire à cause de ses dettes. Pendant les vacances universitaires elle doit toujours trouver un boulot et travailler
40 le plus possible pour avoir un peu d'argent avant la rentrée. Anita explique comment elle a eu ces dettes: «Je ne peux pas résister quand je suis devant une vitrine. Même quand je
45 sais que les articles ne sont pas toujours nécessaires, je dois les acheter tout de suite! Articles de luxe ou produits liés à l'apparence – un sac à main ou de belles chaussures, des
50 parfums ou des bijoux – je les vois, j'en remplis mon panier et je passe à la caisse. Le problème c'est qu'il y a maintenant trop de facilité de paiement quand on paie ses achats
55 avec une carte. Je n'ai qu'à sortir ma carte de crédit pour avoir ce que je veux.» Récemment, Anita a coupé en deux ses cartes et a parlé à un conseiller à la fac qui l'aide à gérer ses
60 affaires.

«Notre société nous encourage à acheter sans penser. Autrefois, le travailleur recevait une enveloppe avec son salaire dedans. Il savait
65 exactement combien il pouvait dépenser. On achetait les choses parce qu'on en avait besoin. Aujourd'hui, l'argent est invisible» dit Anita.

### Les principales dettes des étudiants
70

Pour la plupart des étudiants, leurs ennuis financiers commencent avec un contrat de téléphone portable qu'ils ont du mal à respecter. Avant
75 d'entrer dans un contrat de longue durée, il y a quelques précautions utiles à prendre. Voici quelques conseils qu'offre un spécialiste en marketing jeunesse.

«Tout d'abord, renseignez-vous
80 avant d' acheter pour ne pas sauter sur la première offre. Négociez et obtenez le meilleur service et le meilleur prix. Et deuxièmement, rappelez-vous que votre situation financière peut
85 changer, et que l'argent que vous avez

gagné ne durera pas pour toujours. Prenez soin de ne pas avoir de paiements mensuels que vous aurez 90 des difficultés à payer.»

**Et quelques suggestions pour les parents.**

Les parents ont eux aussi des responsabilités. «Techniquement, un jeune de 17 ans peut signer un contrat 95 de téléphone portable,» affirme un des experts, «mais il ne faut pas hésiter à parler de finances avec son ado. Discutez avec eux des coûts du téléphone portable, et si nécessaire 100 établissez des règles strictes sur son utilisation. C'est comme ça qu'on évitera de gros problèmes plus tard.»

[1] lorgner = to eye; to look at

## QUESTIONS

*Marks*

1. Businesses try hard to capture the "youth market" in the period after the summer holidays. (lines 1–31)

   (*a*) Why do businesses choose this particular period to target young people? 2

   (*b*) What promises do the advertising leaflets seem to make? 2

   (*c*) What is the "golden rule" of marketing? 1

   (*d*) Why are young people, in particular, attracted to this sort of advertising? 3

2. Anita is an example of a young person who has fallen into debt. (lines 32–68)

   (*a*) How do her debts prevent Anita from doing what she wants? 1

   (*b*) She explains how she got into so much debt. How did it happen? 3

   (*c*) What problem does Anita see with shopping nowadays? 1

   (*d*) What steps has she taken recently to get out of debt? 2

3. Mobile phone contracts are a common cause of young people's debts. (lines 69–103)

   (*a*) How should young people ensure they get the best deal? 2

   (*b*) What should they try to avoid? 1

   (*c*) What can parents do to help their child avoid making an expensive mistake? 2

   **(20)**

4. Translate into English:

   Notre société . . . dit Anita (lines 61–68) 10

   **(30)**

**[Turn over for SECTION II on *Page four***

## SECTION II—DIRECTED WRITING

*Marks*

Last year you were selected to go on a three-month visit to a town in France where you stayed with a French family.

On your return you have been asked to write an account of your experiences **in French** for inclusion in the foreign language section of your school/college magazine.

**You must include** the following information and **you should try to add** other relevant details:

- when you went **and** how you got there
- where the town was situated **and** what it was like
- how you got on with the French family
- some of the things you did during your three-month stay
- what you found to be different about living in France
- whether you feel it is a good idea to spend three months living with a French family.

**Your account should be 150–180 words in length.**

**Marks will be deducted for any area of information that is omitted.**            **(15)**

*[END OF QUESTION PAPER]*

# X059/303

NATIONAL
QUALIFICATIONS
2010

TUESDAY, 18 MAY
11.00 AM – 12.00 NOON

FRENCH
HIGHER
Listening Transcript

**This paper must not be seen by any candidate.**

The material overleaf is provided for use in an emergency only (eg the recording or equipment proving faulty) or where permission has been given in advance by SQA for the material to be read to candidates with additional support needs. The material must be read exactly as printed.

---

**Instructions to reader(s):**

The dialogue below should be read in approximately 4 minutes. On completion of the first reading, pause for two minutes, then read the dialogue a second time.

Where special arrangements have been agreed in advance to allow the reading of the material, those sections marked **(f)** should be read by a female speaker and those marked **(m)** by a male.

**Candidates have two minutes to study the questions before the transcript is read.**

---

*Jean is talking to Annie who has just returned from holiday.*

**(m)**  **Vous venez de passer les vacances avec vos copines pour la première fois, n'est-ce pas?**

**(f)**  Oui, je suis allée en Espagne avec mes copines. C'était la première fois que nous partions seules sans parents et c'était fantastique! Nous avons fait toutes les réservations nous-mêmes.

**(m)**  **Vous étiez combien dans le groupe?**

**(f)**  On était quatre – quatre filles. Nous nous sommes bien amusées car nous sommes du même âge et dans la même classe et donc nous nous sommes bien entendues ensemble. Nous avons fait des économies pendant un an pour pouvoir partir. Voilà pourquoi on a loué un appartement. C'était moins cher.

**(m)**  **Et vous avez aimé ça, votre appartement?**

**(f)**  Ah oui. Nous n'étions pas obligées de nous lever trop tôt le matin pour le petit déjeuner comme dans un hôtel, et le soir nous pouvions jouer de la musique en bavardant presque toute la nuit. Il y avait même un petit balcon qui donnait sur la piscine et les jardins.

**(m)**  **Il y avait d' autres avantages?**

**(f)**  Oui. On dépense moins pour la nourriture quand on est dans un appartement car on a la possibilité de préparer des plats simples. Ça coûte assez cher de toujours manger au restaurant.

**(m)**  **Et est-ce que vous avez parlé beaucoup espagnol?**

**(f)**  Ah oui, nous avons essayé de perfectionner notre langue. On a fait des efforts pour parler espagnol, d'abord avec la serveuse dans un petit café du coin où on mangeait, et plus tard, le soir, quand on allait en boîte et bavardait avec les garçons qu'on y rencontrait! Mais tout le monde a trouvé notre accent espagnol très amusant.

**(m)** **Vous préférez les vacances comme ça avec vos copines?**

**(f)** Oui, avec les copines on peut choisir ce qu'on veut faire. On peut faire ce qu'on veut quand on veut. Mais, d'un autre côté, quand on part en famille, on a moins de préparatifs à faire, et on se sent plus en sécurité quand les parents sont là.

**(m)** **Donc, vous aimez aussi partir en vacances avec les parents?**

**(f)** Oh, je ne sais pas, parce qu'il y a aussi des inconvénients. C'est surtout à cause de mon père. Il insiste pour qu'on se lève toujours de bonne heure. Et il veut toujours être actif et faire quelque chose. Il s'amuse à faire des photos tout le temps. Il déteste s'asseoir sur la plage.

**(m)** **Alors vous allez partir sans parents à l'avenir?**

**(f)** Au contraire! L'été prochain je ferai un grand voyage en Australie avec mes parents. Ma cousine se marie là-bas et nous a invités. Après le mariage, je voudrais visiter Sydney car on dit que c'est une ville merveilleuse. Je voudrais faire du ski nautique dans la baie, ou peut-être même faire un saut à l'élastique! On ne sait jamais!

Vous voyez – les parents sont toujours utiles quand il s'agit de payer!

*[END OF TRANSCRIPT]*

[BLANK PAGE]

FOR OFFICIAL USE

| | | | | | |
|---|---|---|---|---|---|

| Examiner's Marks | |
|---|---|
| A | |
| B | |

Total Mark

# X059/302

NATIONAL
QUALIFICATIONS
2010

TUESDAY, 18 MAY
11.00 AM – 12.00 NOON

FRENCH
HIGHER
Listening/Writing

**Fill in these boxes and read what is printed below.**

Full name of centre

Town

Forename(s)

Surname

Date of birth

Day    Month    Year    Scottish candidate number    Number of seat

**Do not open this paper until told to do so.**

Answer Section A **in English** and Section B **in French**.

**Section A**

Listen carefully to the recording with a view to answering, **in English**, the questions printed in this answer book.   Write your answers **clearly and legibly** in the spaces provided after each question.

**You will have 2 minutes to study the questions before hearing the dialogue for the first time.**

The dialogue will be played **twice**, with an interval of 2 minutes between the two playings.

You may make notes at any time but only in this answer book. **Score out any notes before you hand in the book.**

Move on to Section B when you have completed Section A: you will **not** be told when to do this.

**Section B**

**Do not** write your response in this book: **use the 4 page lined answer sheet**.

You will be told to insert the answer sheet inside this book before handing in your work.

You may consult a French dictionary at any time during **both** sections.

Before leaving the examination room you must give this book to the Invigilator. If you do not, you may lose all the marks for this paper.

DO NOT
WRITE IN
THIS
MARGIN

**Section A**

*Marks*

Jean is talking to Annie who has just returned from holiday.

1. What was unusual about this holiday for Annie?    **1**

2. Why had her group got on so well together?    **2**

3. How had they prepared for the holiday?    **1**

4. What did they like about their flat?    **3**

5. How did living in a flat save them money?    **1**

*Marks*

**6.**   (*a*)   What opportunities did they have to practise their Spanish?    **2**

     (*b*)   How did people react to their efforts?    **1**

**7.**   (*a*)   What did she especially like about holidays with her friends?    **1**

     (*b*)   Name **one** advantage of going on holiday with parents that she mentions.    **1**

**8.**   What does she dislike about going on holiday with her dad?    **3**

**9.**   (*a*)   What plans does she have for next year's holiday?    **2**

     (*b*)   Why is she looking forward to visiting Sydney?    **2**

                                        **(20)**

**[Turn over for Section B on *Page four***

DO NOT
WRITE IN
THIS
MARGIN

*Marks*

**Section B**

Annie nous parle des vacances.

Quelles sont vos vacances idéales? Avec ou sans parents? Actives ou relaxantes? Donnez vos raisons.

Ecrivez 120-150 mots en français pour exprimer vos idées.

**10**

**(30)**

### USE THE 4 PAGE LINED ANSWER SHEET FOR YOUR ANSWER TO SECTION B

*[END OF QUESTION PAPER]*

HIGHER

2011

[BLANK PAGE]

# X059/301

NATIONAL
QUALIFICATIONS
2011

TUESDAY, 17 MAY
9.00 AM – 10.40 AM

FRENCH
HIGHER
Reading and
Directed Writing

45 marks are allocated to this paper. The value attached to each question is shown after each question.

You should spend approximately one hour on Section I and 40 minutes on Section II.

You may use a French dictionary.

# SECTION I—READING

Read the whole article carefully and then answer **in English** the questions which follow it.

In this article Hugo Girard, a famous Canadian strongman, talks about his life and his plans to retire from the world of competition.

## Hugo Girard prend sa retraite des compétitions d'hommes forts

Après plus de dix ans de compétitions sur la scène internationale, Hugo Girard, un athlète de force, vient d'annoncer sa
5　retraite. Ce géant à la force surhumaine, qui soulève facilement des roches lourdes de cent kilos et qui tire des camions, quitte le monde des hommes forts la tête haute. «Je crois
10　que j'ai gagné le respect des gens du Canada et que je laisse derrière moi l'image d'un homme qui a des valeurs et des principes,» dit-il. «Pour moi, ça, c'est le plus important.»

15　**Il faut faire les bons choix**

Depuis son enfance, Hugo Girard a une passion pour l'entraînement physique. A l'âge de dix ans, il regardait son père s'entraîner dans leur
20　maison. «Pour moi, mon père était l'homme le plus fort du monde, et je rêvais de devenir aussi fort que lui,» raconte Hugo. «Aussi, je lisais beaucoup de bandes dessinées et je
25　m'imaginais être le superhéros.

Mais j'ai fait un bon choix de carrière quand je suis devenu policier dans la ville de Gatineau avant de faire le saut dans le monde des hommes
30　forts. On m'a permis de prendre un congé sans solde et j'ai toujours gardé en tête que j'avais une carrière si je ne réussissais pas dans la compétition.»

**La motivation**

35　Hugo a repoussé ses limites tout au long de sa vie, et c'est cette motivation de réussir qui a plus impressionné son public. «Je suis comme le boxeur qui tombe au tapis et qui a deux choix:
40　rester à terre ou se relever. Moi, j'ai été blessé plusieurs fois, mais j'ai toujours su trouver le courage

nécessaire pour continuer la compétition et battre des records. La
45　vie est faite d'obstacles, de bons moments et de moins bons moments, mais il faut savoir passer au travers et s'accrocher à ses rêves.»

C'est pour ça que Hugo Girard donne des conférences sur la
50　motivation aux étudiants des écoles secondaires depuis le début de sa carrière d'homme fort. «À travers mon message, je souhaite encourager les jeunes à se surpasser et surtout à croire
55　en eux-mêmes. Je veux leur faire voir qu'on peut réussir de grandes choses tout en étant quelqu'un de bien ordinaire. Il faut seulement faire les bons choix et travailler fort pour
60　réaliser son rêve.»

**Les préjugés**

Mais même s'il est aujourd'hui l'idole de plusieurs athlètes, Hugo Girard a vécu les préjugés réservés aux
65　sportifs dès son adolescence. «L'image de l'homme sportif typique – beaucoup de talent et pas beaucoup de cerveau – m'a forcé à montrer au public que j'étais autre chose qu'un
70　homme fort. Il y en a plein d'autres qui peuvent soulever une pierre lourde, mais trouver la motivation pour être champion canadien six fois, ça c'est autre chose.»
75

**Changer les perceptions**

Maintenant de retour à la vie normale, Hugo sait qu'il y aura la difficulté d'une période d'adaptation, mais il y fera face au moment venu.
80　Pour le moment, il ne pense qu'à passer plus de temps avec ses proches, et surtout avec son fils Tyles qui

entre à la prématernelle cette année.
85 «Mon fils a changé ma perception de la
vie. Aujourd'hui, je sais qu' il y a des
choses plus importantes que d'être
toujours le premier dans tout ce qu'on
fait. A vrai dire, je le savais avant,
90 mais mon fils me l'a fait réaliser
pleinement.»

Et voilà pourquoi Hugo Girard
reprendra son uniforme de policier
dans la Sûreté Municipale de Gatineau
le 15 octobre prochain. «À long terme, 95
j'aimerais travailler dans le secteur des
communications et des relations
publiques de la police. Après tout,
c'est ce que je fais depuis dix ans.»

## QUESTIONS

*Marks*

1. Hugo Girard believes he has had a successful career as a strongman. (lines 1–14)

   (*a*) What examples are given of Hugo's feats of strength? **2**

   (*b*) Why does he feel proud of himself? **2**

2. He has been careful when planning out his career. (lines 15–33)

   (*a*) What were his ambitions when he was a boy? Mention **two** things. **2**

   (*b*) Why was it a good decision to join the police? Give any **one** reason. **1**

3. Self-motivation is one of his key qualities. (lines 34–61)

   (*a*) How has Hugo taken inspiration from boxers? **2**

   (*b*) What is his approach to the difficulties of life? **2**

   (*c*) What effect does he hope that his seminars will have upon young people? **3**

4. According to Hugo, people often have negative views of sportsmen and women. (lines 62–75)

   (*a*) What does he think is the view that people have of a typical sportsman? **1**

   (*b*) How does he think that he has proved himself different from most athletes? **1**

5. He is now about to embark on a new lifestyle. (lines 76–99)

   (*a*) What are his plans for the immediate future? **1**

   (*b*) What is he going to do in October? **1**

   (*c*) What is his long-term ambition, and why? **2**

   **(20)**

6. Translate into English:

   "Mon fils a changé . . . me l'a fait réaliser pleinement." (lines 85–91) **10**

   **(30)**

**[Turn over for SECTION II on *Page four***

## SECTION II—DIRECTED WRITING

*Marks*

Last summer, you spent 2 months in France, working in a holiday camp for French schoolchildren (une colonie de vacances), where you helped with the activities organised for them. During your stay, you shared accommodation with other student helpers.

On your return from the visit, you have been asked to write an account of your experiences **in French** for inclusion in the foreign language section of your school/college magazine.

**You must include** the following information and **you should try to add** other relevant details:

- where the camp was **and** how you travelled there
- how you found out about the job
- what you did to help with activities for the children
- what you thought of sharing your accommodation with other students
- what opportunities you had to visit other parts of France
- why you would or would not recommend this type of experience to others.

**Your account should be 150–180 words in length.**

**Marks will be deducted for any area of information that is omitted.**

(15)

*[END OF QUESTION PAPER]*

# X059/303

| | | |
|---|---|---|
| NATIONAL QUALIFICATIONS 2011 | TUESDAY, 17 MAY 11.00 AM – 12.00 NOON | FRENCH HIGHER Listening Transcript |

**This paper must not be seen by any candidate.**

The material overleaf is provided for use in an emergency only (eg the recording or equipment proving faulty) or where permission has been given in advance by SQA for the material to be read to candidates with additional support needs.  The material must be read exactly as printed.

**Instructions to reader(s):**

The dialogue below should be read in approximately 4 minutes. On completion of the first reading, pause for two minutes, then read the dialogue a second time.

Where special arrangements have been agreed in advance to allow the reading of the material, those sections marked **(f)** should be read by a female speaker and those marked **(m)** by a male.

**Candidates have two minutes to study the questions before the transcript is read.**

*Anaïs is in the final year in her lycée and she is discussing what lies ahead for her.*

**(m)** **Anaïs, est-ce que ton année de terminale se passe bien?**

**(f)** Oui, ça se passe bien. D'abord, en terminale, on étudie seulement les cours qui nous intéressent: par exemple je ne fais plus de sciences parce que j'étudie la littérature. Et en plus, en France on a le droit de quitter l'établissement quand on veut, si on n'a pas classe, sans demander à personne. Notre lycée est à côté d'une forêt, donc on peut aller se promener dans la forêt. Certains élèves préfèrent traîner dans la cour, tandis que d'autres qui n'habitent pas très loin du lycée choisissent de rentrer à la maison.

**(m)** **La pensée des examens du bac ne t'inquiète pas?**

**(f)** Non, j'étudie la littérature et je suis forte dans cette matière. Je ne voudrais absolument pas rater mon bac parce qu'en ce cas – là, si on n'a pas de bonnes notes au bac, on doit, soit recommencer l'année, soit arrêter les études. Mais je trouverais ça idiot si on arrêtait après six longues années d'études.

**(m)** **Et ensuite il faut prendre des décisions pour l'avenir. Y a-t-il quelqu'un qui peut vous aider?**

**(f)** Je n'ai pas encore décidé quelle carrière je veux faire, mais il y a des conseillers d'orientation pour nous aider. Heureusement, il y a un conseiller dans tous les lycées, et si on veut lui parler, on peut tout simplement lui demander un rendez-vous. Le conseiller peut mieux nous aider car il nous connaît et il a toutes nos notes.

**(m)** **A ton avis, est-ce que les jeunes ont beaucoup de stress maintenant?**

**(f)** Oui, mais surtout ceux qui vont à l'université, et en particulier sur le plan financier où on a plus de dettes. Mes amis qui sont déjà à la fac m'ont parlé des difficultés à trouver un appartement à un prix raisonnable et à payer les transports en commun. On a pas mal de difficultés à se débrouiller seul si vos parents n'ont pas les moyens de vous aider. Mais, moi, j'ai de la chance parce que mes parents m'ont dit qu'ils vont me donner 300 euros tous les mois. En plus, quand je rentrerai chez eux en voiture ils me payeront l'essence.

**(m)**    **Est-ce que tu dirais qu'il y a beaucoup de tentations à éviter quand on est étudiant?**

**(f)**    Oui, il y a beaucoup de tentations, surtout pour les étudiants d'université. A mon avis, les plus dangereuses sont la drogue et faire trop la fête. On a toujours des copains qui fument de la drogue et qui font la fête tout le temps, et ce sont deux habitudes qu'il faut éviter à tout prix. Enfin, la drogue, ça peut avoir de mauvaises conséquences pour la santé et si l'on fait la fête tout le temps, on est trop fatigué pour bien travailler.

**(m)**    **Quand tu auras fini tes études à la fac, as-tu l'intention de chercher un emploi immédiatement?**

**(f)**    Bien sûr, à l'avenir je voudrais m'installer quelque part en France et avoir un métier qui me plaît et une maison à la campagne où je pourrais apprécier mon temps libre. Mais avant cela j'ai l'intention de prendre une année sabbatique et de visiter d'autres pays. Bien sûr que tout cela va me coûter encore plus d'argent, et en conséquence, je voudrais rembourser mes dettes le plus tôt possible.

*[END OF TRANSCRIPT]*

[BLANK PAGE]

FOR OFFICIAL USE

| | | | | | |
|---|---|---|---|---|---|
| | | | | | |

Examiner's Marks

| A | |
|---|---|
| B | |

Total Mark

# X059/302

NATIONAL
QUALIFICATIONS
2011

TUESDAY, 17 MAY
11.00 AM – 12.00 NOON

FRENCH
HIGHER
Listening/Writing

**Fill in these boxes and read what is printed below.**

Full name of centre

Town

Forename(s)

Surname

Date of birth

Day    Month    Year      Scottish candidate number      Number of seat

**Do not open this paper until told to do so.**

Answer Section A **in English** and Section B **in French**.

**Section A**

Listen carefully to the recording with a view to answering, **in English**, the questions printed in this answer book. Write your answers **clearly and legibly** in the spaces provided after each question.

**You will have 2 minutes to study the questions before hearing the dialogue for the first time.**

The dialogue will be played **twice**, with an interval of 2 minutes between the two playings.

You may make notes at any time but only in this answer book. **Score out any notes before you hand in the book.**

Move on to Section B when you have completed Section A: you will **not** be told when to do this.

**Section B**

**Do not** write your response in this book: **use the 4 page lined answer sheet**.

You will be told to insert the answer sheet inside this book before handing in your work.

You may consult a French dictionary at any time during **both** sections.

Before leaving the examination room you must give this book to the Invigilator. If you do not, you may lose all the marks for this paper.

## Section A

*Marks*

Anaïs is in the final year in her lycée and she is discussing what lies ahead for her.

1. (*a*) What two things does Anaïs like about being in "terminale"?  **2**

   (*b*) How might students spend their free time during the school day?  **2**

2. (*a*) Why is she not too worried about the "bac" exam?  **1**

   (*b*) What options are there for those students who do not pass?  **2**

3. (*a*) Why is it easy to talk to a careers adviser?  **2**

   (*b*) Why are they in a good position to help you?  **1**

*Marks*

**4.** Anaïs talks about young people's money worries.

   (*a*) Mention two ways in which young people spend their money.   **2**

   (*b*) How do her own parents plan to help her financially?   **2**

**5.** Anaïs mentions two dangers facing students. What are they and what are their consequences?   **2**

**6.** At the end of her studies, what are her long-term plans?   **2**

**7.** (*a*) What are her immediate plans?   **1**

   (*b*) What consequences will this have for her?   **1**

**(20)**

**[Turn over for Section B on *Page four***

*Marks*

**Section B**

Anaïs nous a parlé de ses expériences au lycée et des problèmes des jeunes. Et vous, est-ce que vous êtes content(e) dans votre lycée/collège? A votre avis, quelles sont les inquiétudes typiques des jeunes personnes d'aujourd'hui?

Ecrivez 120–150 mots en français pour exprimer vos idées.

**10**

**(30)**

**USE THE 4 PAGE LINED ANSWER SHEET FOR YOUR ANSWER TO SECTION B**

*[END OF QUESTION PAPER]*

HIGHER

2012

[BLANK PAGE]

# X059/12/01

NATIONAL
QUALIFICATIONS
2012

THURSDAY, 24 MAY
9.00 AM – 10.40 AM

FRENCH
HIGHER
Reading and
Directed Writing

45 marks are allocated to this paper. The value attached to each question is shown after each question.

You should spend approximately one hour on Section I and 40 minutes on Section II.

You may use a French dictionary.

## SECTION 1 – READING

Read the whole article carefully and then answer **in English** the questions which follow it.

In this passage Florence is talking about her job with the charity organisation 'Petits Princes', which tries to make life happier for children who are ill.

### Les Petits Princes

De nos jours un pourcentage important de la population se sent assez stressé par le train-train quotidien. On se lève très tôt pour
5  lutter contre la circulation ou bien on est coincé dans le métro avec des centaines de personnes qui font exactement la même chose. Quand on rentre enfin à la maison familiale
10  vers 20 heures, on trouve le partenaire fatigué aussi après une longue journée de travail pareil. Mais il y a certains gens qui ont réussi à s'échapper de cette situation de plus en plus
15  stressante.

Il y a cinq ans, Florence avait un poste de responsabilité bien payé dans le marketing; maintenant, elle est bénévole à l'association
20  'Petits Princes', qui aide les enfants gravement malades à réaliser leurs rêves.

### «J'apporte des moments de bonheur.»

25  Elle raconte son histoire avec passion. «Un jour, j'en ai eu assez de promouvoir des savons. Je voulais donner un autre sens à ma vie.» En quête d'idées sur internet, elle tombe
30  sur le site 'Petits Princes'. «C'était exactement ce que je cherchais,» dit-elle, les yeux brillants, «car je savais que j'allais pouvoir y être utile. Je ne me suis pas trompée!»

35  Et la différence qu'elle fait est facile à voir. Comme tous les bénévoles, elle a à sa charge quarante enfants malades—ses 'petits princes et princesses'—qu'elle suit durant
40  toute leur maladie. Pour fêter leur anniversaire, elle les emmène au spectacle; quand ils se sentent tristes, elle leur apporte sourires et réconfort.

Donc, chaque mois, elle part avec l'un d'eux pour lui offrir un petit moment
45  de bonheur. «Ils ne demandent pas la lune,» nous dit-elle. «Ils sont réalistes et, en règle générale, ont les mêmes passions que tous les enfants!»

### Florence se dépense sans compter.
50

«On ne trouvera pas de pessimisme dans notre association,» explique-t-elle. «Certes, il est vrai qu'il y a des bas et des hauts. Souvent on est
55  confronté à la maladie et à la douleur. Mais par contre on sait toujours qu'on donne de l'espoir et du rêve.» Quand on demande à Florence quels sont les plus beaux souhaits qu'elle a
60  réalisés, elle hésite parce qu'il y en a tant. Elle raconte . . . les enfants qui voulaient voir le Père Noël et qu'elle a emmenés à son atelier en Laponie; ce petit garçon passionné de dauphins
65  qui est parti avec elle en Floride; cette petite fille qui a galopé sur les chevaux en Provence avec ses frères et sœurs . . . Florence pourrait parler des heures de tous ces enfants qui
70  ont pu, le temps d'un rêve, oublier leur maladie. Elle reprend la parole: «Réaliser un rêve donne souvent à l'enfant la force de se battre contre la maladie et d'accepter les traitements,
75  parfois très lourds.»

### Une vie difficile, mais réussie

Aujourd'hui, Florence partage son temps entre l'association et sa famille: «J'ai la chance incroyable d'avoir trouvé un équilibre: pouvoir
80  me consacrer à mes deux filles et faire une activité qui me passionne!» s'enthousiasme-t-elle. Elle se rend deux jours par semaine à l'association pour recevoir les enfants et les
85  familles et se réunir avec les autres

bénévoles. «Heureusement nous avons le soutien d'un psychologue,» précise-t-elle. «C'est indispensable,
90 car il y a parfois des moments difficiles pour les bénévoles. Dans cette association on verse des larmes mais surtout de joie. Et si mes filles me demandent parfois, 'Mais pourquoi n'es–tu pas payée pour ce que tu fais?' 95 je leur réponds alors que mon salaire, c'est le sourire de l'enfant! »

## Questions
*Marks*

1. Nowadays a large number of people are stressed by the routine of their working day. (lines 1–22)

   (*a*) How does the author show how stressful the journey to work can be? **2**

   (*b*) When someone returns home from work, what situation might he or she find? **1**

   (*c*) What does the author say about Florence's previous job in marketing? **1**

2. Florence speaks about her current job as a volunteer with 'Petits Princes'. (lines 23–43)

   (*a*) What motivated her to change job? **2**

   (*b*) What did she feel when she saw the job advertised on the 'Petits Princes' website? Mention any **one** thing. **1**

   (*c*) Give **two** examples of how she can make a child's life better. **2**

3. Her work with 'Petits Princes' has both low points and high points. (lines 50–75)

   (*a*) Which low point and which high point does she mention? **2**

   (*b*) What examples does she give of making children's dreams come true? **3**

   (*c*) How can such experiences help an ill child? **2**

4. Florence is now contented with her life. (lines 76–97)

   (*a*) What balance has she achieved in her life? **1**

   (*b*) The organisation employs a psychologist. Why? **1**

   (*c*) What do her daughters sometimes ask her, and how does she answer? **2**

   **(20)**

5. Translate into English:

   « Donc, chaque mois, ... les mêmes passions que tous les enfants!» (lines 44–49) **10**

**[Turn over for SECTION II on *Page four* (30)**

## SECTION II—DIRECTED WRITING

*Marks*

Last summer, you were one of a group of students who went with your school for two weeks' work experience in France.

On your return from the visit, you have been asked to write an account of your experiences **in French** for inclusion in the foreign language section of your school/college website.

**You must include** the following information and **you should try to add** other relevant details:

- how many of you went to France **and** where you went

- what job you did **and** how much you earned

- what you had to do in your work experience

- how you got on with the people that you worked with

- what you liked and/or disliked about the job

- if you would now consider working abroad when you are older.

**Your account should be 150–180 words in length.**

**Marks will be deducted for any area of information that is omitted.**

**(15)**

*[END OF QUESTION PAPER]*

# X059/12/12

NATIONAL
QUALIFICATIONS
2012

THURSDAY, 24 MAY
11.00 AM – 12.00 NOON

**FRENCH
HIGHER**
Listening Transcript

**This paper must not be seen by any candidate.**

The material overleaf is provided for use in an emergency only (eg the recording or equipment proving faulty) or where permission has been given in advance by SQA for the material to be read to candidates with additional support needs.   The material must be read exactly as printed.

**Instructions to reader(s):**

The dialogue below should be read in approximately 4 minutes. On completion of the first reading, pause for two minutes, then read the dialogue a second time.

Where special arrangements have been agreed in advance to allow the reading of the material, those sections marked **(f)** should be read by a female speaker and those marked **(m)** by a male.

**Candidates have two minutes to study the questions before the transcript is read.**

*Annie, a student in a French lycée, has just returned to France after spending a term in a Scottish school as part of an exchange. Here she tells us about her experiences.*

**(m)    Annie, vous venez de passer trois mois en Ecosse. Est-ce que vous avez profité de votre séjour là-bas?**

**(f)**    Oui. Le plus grand avantage c'est que j'ai pu améliorer mon anglais. Mais, ce n'est pas surprenant, parce que quand on est tout seul dans un pays et quand on ne connaît personne, on n'a pas d'autre choix que de parler avec les gens, et on apprend la langue en bavardant.

**(m)    Est-ce qu'il y avait d'autres avantages?**

**(f)**    Un deuxième avantage c'était de voir comment les gens vivent en Ecosse, par exemple ce qu'ils font dans leur temps libre.

**(m)    Est-ce que vous avez trouvé beaucoup de différences entre la vie en Ecosse et la vie en France?**

**(f)**    Alors, j'ai trouvé que la façon de manger est très différente. En France nous avons deux repas principaux—le déjeuner et le dîner—alors qu'en Ecosse il me semble qu'on mange plus souvent: on grignote presque toute la journée! J'ai donc changé mes propres habitudes: à midi en France je mange toujours à la cantine du lycée; quand j'étais en Ecosse je sortais en ville acheter quelque chose dans un magasin.

**(m)    Qu'est-ce que vous avez pensé de la vie scolaire en Ecosse?**

**(f)**    Je préfère la journée scolaire en Ecosse parce que je pouvais rentrer à la maison à quinze heures trente tandis qu'en France je ne rentre qu'à dix-sept heures et quelquefois même plus tard. En plus, j'avais moins de devoirs en Ecosse!

**(m)    Pendant ce long séjour, y avait-il des moments difficiles?**

**(f)**    Oui. Quelquefois je me sentais triste simplement parce que j'avais laissé mes amis en France. C'est normal, n'est-ce pas? Je faisais des efforts pour me faire des amis écossais mais quand on ne parle pas bien la langue, l'accent écossais est parfois difficile à comprendre.

**(m)    Qu'est-ce que vous avez fait pour vous adapter à la vie en Ecosse?**

**(f)**    Heureusement, j'étais résolue à réussir et j'ai fait un grand effort pour faire beaucoup de connaissances. La famille chez qui je logeais était très sympa et puis au lycée j'ai rencontré beaucoup de gens de mon âge. Le plus important est de se faire des amis. Je me suis inscrite dans toutes sortes de clubs: j'ai participé à des sports d'équipe et j'ai commencé à chanter dans une chorale, ce qui me plaisait beaucoup. Les clubs sont un excellent moyen de connaître les gens.

**(m)** **Et finalement, êtes-vous contente d'avoir passé ce trimestre en Ecosse?**

**(f)** Oui, parce que je crois que j'ai beaucoup gagné en confiance en moi, et j'ai appris à  me débrouiller seule. Voilà deux choses très importantes pour la vie.  Je n'oublierai jamais les gens que j'ai connus là-bas, et les choses que j'ai faites, mais, en fin de compte, il faut avouer que j'étais bien contente de rentrer en France et de revoir mes amis et ma famille!

*[END OF TRANSCRIPT]*

[BLANK PAGE]

FOR OFFICIAL USE

| | | | | | |
|---|---|---|---|---|---|
| | | | | | |

| Examiner's Marks | |
|---|---|
| A | |
| B | |

Total Mark

# X059/12/02

NATIONAL
QUALIFICATIONS
2012

THURSDAY, 24 MAY
11.00 AM – 12.00 NOON

FRENCH
HIGHER
Listening/Writing

**Fill in these boxes and read what is printed below.**

Full name of centre

Town

Forename(s)

Surname

Date of birth

Day    Month    Year        Scottish candidate number        Number of seat

**Do not open this paper until told to do so.**

Answer Section A **in English** and Section B **in French**.

**Section A**

Listen carefully to the recording with a view to answering, **in English**, the questions printed in this answer book. Write your answers **clearly and legibly** in the spaces provided after each question.

**You will have 2 minutes to study the questions before hearing the dialogue for the first time.**

The dialogue will be played **twice**, with an interval of 2 minutes between the two playings.

You may make notes at any time but only in this answer book. **Score out any notes before you hand in the book.**

Move on to Section B when you have completed Section A: you will **not** be told when to do this.

**Section B**

**Do not** write your response in this book: **use the 4 page lined answer sheet**.

You will be told to insert the answer sheet inside this book before handing in your work.

You may consult a French dictionary at any time during **both** sections.

Before leaving the examination room you must give this book to the Invigilator. If you do not, you may lose all the marks for this paper.

*Marks*

## Section A

Annie, a student in a French lycée, has just returned to France after spending a term in a Scottish school as part of an exchange. Here she tells us about her experiences.

1. (*a*) What was the biggest advantage for Annie of spending three months in Scotland?

1

(*b*) Why was it not surprising that this should happen?

2

2. What second advantage does she mention?

1

3. (*a*) What differences in eating habits did she find between Scotland and France?

2

(*b*) How did her lunchtime eating habits change when she was in Scotland?

2

4. What **two** things did she particularly like about Scottish schools?

2

*Marks*

5. (*a*) Why did Annie sometimes feel sad?

1

(*b*) What made it difficult for her to make friends at first?

2

6. (*a*) Who helped her to get over this initial difficulty?

2

(*b*) What else did she do to get to know people?

2

7. (*a*) In what **two** ways did she benefit from her stay?

2

(*b*) What is her final comment on her experiences?

1

(20)

[**Turn over for Section B on** *Page four*

*Marks*

**Section B**

Annie nous a expliqué combien ses amis lui ont manqué quand elle était en Ecosse.

Et vous, aimez-vous passer beaucoup de temps avec les copains, ou est-ce que vous préférez être seul(e) de temps en temps?  A votre avis, quelles sont les qualités d'un(e) bon(ne) ami(e)?

Ecrivez 120—150 mots en français pour exprimer vos idées.    **10**

**(30)**

**USE THE 4 PAGE LINED ANSWER SHEET FOR YOUR ANSWER TO SECTION B**

*[END OF QUESTION PAPER]*

[BLANK PAGE]

# X059/12/01

| | | |
|---|---|---|
| NATIONAL QUALIFICATIONS 2013 | WEDNESDAY, 29 MAY 9.00 AM – 10.40 AM | FRENCH HIGHER Reading and Directed Writing |

45 marks are allocated to this paper.  The value attached to each question is shown after each question.

You should spend approximately one hour on Section I and 40 minutes on Section II.

You may use a French dictionary.

## SECTION 1 – READING

Read the whole article carefully and then answer **in English** the questions which follow it.

In this article the author talks about owning a second home in the countryside.

### Une maison de campagne pour se faire des souvenirs.

Comme 10% des Français, Michèle Manceaux, journaliste et écrivain, a acheté une résidence secondaire, à Rambouillet, à 35 km
5 de Paris. «Les semaines sont denses et fatigantes: travail, ménage, famille. Quand on a tant de responsabilités pendant la semaine il faut profiter au maximum des week-ends pour
10 vivre des moments précieux et pour changer d'air. C'est pour ça qu'on a acheté une maison à la campagne» dit Michèle.

### Un besoin de racines

15 Les maisons de campagne sont souvent achetées par des citadins qui sont locataires. Michèle raconte «Je ne suis pas née dans une famille assez riche pour posséder
20 une maison de famille. Comme la plupart des Français j'ai grandi dans un appartement que mes parents louaient. Voilà pourquoi sans doute j'ai souhaité devenir propriétaire de
25 quelques mètres carrés sur le sol de la France». Psychologue et auteur, Patrick Estrade confirme: «Avoir une maison de campagne, c'est dire qu'on a des racines quelque part.»

30 ### Une qualité de vie retrouvée

Michèle a acheté sa maison après la naissance de sa première fille. «Mon mari a passé son enfance à la campagne. Alors il a toujours aimé
35 la vie en plein air et il a voulu que sa fille échappe à la pollution de la grande ville. En plus nous sommes locataires de notre appartement à Paris, mais nous n'aurons jamais
40 assez d'argent pour y acheter un appartement. Alors nous avons choisi d'acheter une maison à 150 km de Paris.» Un choix que Michèle et son mari, Philippe, ne regrettent pas. Pour eux leur maison principale 45 c'est celle de la campagne. Tous les week-ends la famille part le vendredi soir et rentre le lundi matin. Une fois arrivés à la maison, ils peuvent passer le temps ensemble. Ils ont même 50 trouvé le temps de jardiner et faire la cuisine.

Pourtant, posséder une résidence secondaire peut aussi apporter des inconvénients. «Tu n'as pas peur 55 des bouchons le dimanche soir? Tu ne passes pas ton temps à faire les courses et le ménage?» Ce sont des questions que posent des amis et c'est vrai . . . Posséder une maison 60 de campagne implique faire des kilomètres en voiture, avec risque d'embouteillages. En plus il faut entretenir la maison. Deux maisons c'est deux fois plus de boulot! Mais 65 sur place on oublie ces problèmes. Michèle raconte. «On a le sentiment de se retrouver au calme, loin du stress et de la vie de tous les jours.»

C'est une vie plus simple. L'hiver 70 on allume le feu et on se couche sur le canapé, un livre à la main, une tasse de thé à proximité. A la campagne tout est permis et les enfants sont libres—ça ne fait rien 75 s'ils font du bruit, quand il n'y a pas de voisins. Pendant la journée les enfants disparaissent des heures dans le jardin ou partent faire de grandes balades à vélo ou bien ils 80 jouent dans le grenier. Michèle et son mari n'ont pas voulu la télé. Le soir toute la famille se retrouve autour des jeux de société. C'est une parenthèse dans une vie intense. 85

**Au bout de quelque temps ça change**

Cependant, à partir d'un certain âge, les ados rejettent parfois ce qu'ils ont
90 adoré comme enfants. Ils s'ennuient loin de leurs amis et n'espèrent qu'une chose: que les parents partent en week-end à la campagne et leur laissent le champ libre à la maison. C'est à ce
95 moment-là que Michèle a vendu sa maison: «Je commençais à être épuisée de ces allers-retours. Les copains venaient seulement en été, quand ils étaient sûrs d'avoir du beau temps.
Il y avait de gros travaux à faire dans 100 la maison et nous n'aimons pas faire le bricolage. Les enfants ne venaient plus, donc, pour toutes ces raisons, on a décidé de vendre la maison.»

Michèle Manceaux aurait bien 105 gardé sa maison, mais c'était son rêve, pas celui de ses enfants. Alors elle l'a vendue en conservant les souvenirs des jours heureux.

## Questions

*Marks*

1. The author talks about the reasons why people want to own a second home. (lines 1–29)

   (a) What reasons does Michèle Manceaux give for buying a second home?    2

   (b) How did Michèle's upbringing influence her decision to buy a house in the country?    2

   (c) What reason does Patrick Estrade give for people wanting to own a house in the country?    1

2. Michèle and her husband chose to buy a house in the country. (lines 30–69)

   (a) What reasons do they give for this?    3

   (b) What questions do Michèle's friends ask about having a second home in the country?    2

   (c) Despite her friends' concerns, why is Michèle happy with her purchase?    2

3. The family enjoys the simple life in the country. (lines 70–85)

   (a) Why are the children free to do what they like in the country?    1

   (b) How do the children spend their time during the day?    3

   (c) How does the family spend the evenings?    1

4. In the end Michèle decided to sell the house. Why was this? Mention any **three** reasons. (lines 86–109)    3

   (20)

5. Translate into English:

   "Un choix que Michèle...........et faire la cuisine." (lines 43–52)    10

**[Turn over for SECTION II on *Page four***    (30)

## SECTION II—DIRECTED WRITING

*Marks*

You have been asked to be part of a school team taking part in a sports competition in France.

On your return from the visit you have been asked to write a report **in French** for the foreign language section of your school website.

**You must include** the following information and **you should try to add** other relevant details:

- how many people were in your group **and** how you travelled

- where you stayed **and** what you thought about the town

- what you did on the days of the competition

- how you got on with the other teams which were taking part

- what you did in your free time

- what benefits you got from being part of a team competing in France.

**Your report should be 150-180 words in length.**

**Marks will be deducted for any area of information that is omitted.** (15)

*[END OF QUESTION PAPER]*

# X059/12/12

| NATIONAL QUALIFICATIONS 2013 | WEDNESDAY, 29 MAY 11.00 AM – 12.00 NOON | FRENCH HIGHER Listening Transcript |

**This paper must not be seen by any candidate.**

The material overleaf is provided for use in an emergency only (eg the recording or equipment proving faulty) or where permission has been given in advance by SQA for the material to be read to candidates with additional support needs.   The material must be read exactly as printed.

> **Instructions to reader(s):**
>
> The dialogue below should be read in approximately 4½ minutes. On completion of the first reading, pause for two minutes, then read the dialogue a second time.
>
> Where special arrangements have been agreed in advance to allow the reading of the material, those sections marked **(f)** should be read by a female speaker and those marked **(m)** by a male.
>
> **Candidates have two minutes to study the questions before the transcript is read.**

*Marie-Claire talks about holidays she spent at her grandparents' house on the French-speaking island of Martinique in the Caribbean.*

**(m)    Marie-Claire, normalement tu passes les grandes vacances chez tes grands-parents qui habitent à la Martinique. Où se trouve la Martinique exactement?**

**(f)**    La Martinique est une île française qui se trouve aux Caraïbes à trois mille kilomètres des Etats-Unis. Pour y arriver, il faut au moins quatre heures de vol des Etats-Unis.

**(m)    Est ce-que tes parents sont d'origine martiniquaise?**

**(f)**    Ma mère non, mais mon père est né à la Martinique. Il a quitté l'île à l'âge de dix-huit ans pour faire des études de médecine à Paris. Il avait l'intention de retourner à la Martinique, mais il s'est marié avec ma mère et il a trouvé un emploi permanent dans un grand hôpital de la banlieue de Paris. Donc, la famille est restée en France.

**(m)    Pourquoi aimes-tu passer les vacances chez tes grands-parents?**

**(f)**    J'aime passer mes vacances chez eux parce que je ne les vois pas souvent, et ils me gâtent beaucoup quand je leur rends visite. Ils ne viennent pas en France parce que ça coûte trop cher, et, en plus, mon grand-père n'est pas en bonne santé, et le vol est trop long pour lui.

**(m)    Qu'est-ce que tu fais à la Martinique, chez tes grands-parents?**

**(f)**    En général, je passe mon temps à me détendre. Ce que j'aime le plus c'est de me lever de très bonne heure avant qu'il ne fasse trop chaud, et de me promener le long de la plage. A cette heure-là il n'y a personne. L'après-midi je fais aussi un peu de ménage à la maison pour aider ma grand-mère.

**(m)    Et comment est-ce que tu passes tes soirées?**

**(f)**    Je ne sors pas beaucoup le soir parce que mes grands-parents habitent assez loin de la ville et il y a peu de transports en commun. Si je veux aller au cinéma, c'est mon grand-père qui doit m'y emmener en voiture. Donc, je reste normalement à la maison et je bavarde avec mes grands-parents.

**(m)    Qu'est-ce qu'il y a pour les touristes là-bas?**

**(f)**    Il y a plein d'attractions pour les touristes. Par exemple, si on s'intéresse aux sports nautiques, on a un grand choix d'activités. On peut également faire des excursions en bateau ou faire de la plongée sous-marine. D'autres activités qui sont populaires avec les touristes sont des randonnées à l'intérieur du pays ou à la montagne.

**(m)** **Tu trouves que le mode de vie à la Martinique est très différent de la France?**

**(f)** En général oui. Je trouve que les gens sont beaucoup plus ouverts et souriants que les Français. En plus, le rythme de vie est plus lent et plus décontracté. Les gens ne sont pas toujours pressés comme à Paris.

**(m)** **Tu voudrais habiter à la Martinique à l'avenir?**

**(f)** A vrai dire, je ne voudrais pas y habiter. Naturellement, j'aime rendre visite chaque année à mes grands-parents, mais il existe pas mal de problèmes là-bas. Il y a beaucoup de chômage parmi les jeunes et si on trouve un emploi, c'est souvent mal payé et il faut travailler de longues heures.

**(m)** **Qu'est-ce que tu voudrais faire plus tard dans la vie?**

**(f)** J'espère devenir médecin, comme mon père, et si je réussis, je voudrais travailler en Afrique pour aider les gens malades. Je voudrais aussi faire une année sabbatique, soit en Australie soit aux Etats-Unis, pour améliorer ma connaissance de la langue anglaise. Je ne sais pas exactement . . .

*[END OF TRANSCRIPT]*

[BLANK PAGE]

FOR OFFICIAL USE

| | | | | | |
|---|---|---|---|---|---|

| Examiner's Marks | |
|---|---|
| A | |
| B | |

Total Mark

# X059/12/02

NATIONAL QUALIFICATIONS 2013

WEDNESDAY, 29 MAY 11.00 AM – 12.00 NOON

FRENCH HIGHER Listening/Writing

---

**Fill in these boxes and read what is printed below.**

Full name of centre

Town

Forename(s)

Surname

Date of birth

| Day | Month | Year | Scottish candidate number | Number of seat |
|---|---|---|---|---|

**Do not open this paper until told to do so.**

Answer Section A **in English** and Section B **in French**.

**Section A**

Listen carefully to the recording with a view to answering, **in English**, the questions printed in this answer book. Write your answers **clearly and legibly** in the spaces provided after each question.

**You will have 2 minutes to study the questions before hearing the dialogue for the first time.**

The dialogue will be played **twice**, with an interval of 2 minutes between the two playings.

You may make notes at any time but only in this answer book. **Score out any notes before you hand in the book.**

Move on to Section B when you have completed Section A: you will **not** be told when to do this.

**Section B**

**Do not** write your response in this book: **use the 4 page lined answer sheet**.

You will be told to insert the answer sheet inside this book before handing in your work.

You may consult a French dictionary at any time during **both** sections.

Before leaving the examination room you must give this book to the Invigilator. If you do not, you may lose all the marks for this paper.

DO NOT
WRITE
IN THIS
MARGIN

*Marks*

**Section A**

Marie-Claire talks about holidays she spent at her grandparents' house on the French-speaking island of Martinique in the Caribbean.

1. Where exactly is the island of Martinique?

   1

2. Marie-Claire's father left the island at the age of 18. Why did he not return to Martinique?

   2

3. (*a*) Why does Marie-Claire like spending holidays at her grandparents' house?

   2

   (*b*) Apart from the cost of the flight, why do her grandparents not go to France?

   1

4. Marie-Claire talks about what she does in Martinique. Why does she like getting up early when she is there?

   2

DO NOT
WRITE
IN THIS
MARGIN

*Marks*

5. (*a*) Why does she not go out much in the evening?    2

   (*b*) When she stays in, how does she spend her evenings?    1

6. (*a*) What activities are available to tourists in Martinique?    2

   (*b*) What activities are there for tourists who do not want to spend time by the sea?    1

7. Marie-Claire compares life on the island with life in France.  According to her, what are the main differences?  Mention any **two** things.    2

8. Why would she not want to live in Martinique in the future?    2

9. What are her plans for the future?  Mention any **two** things.    2

(20)

**[Turn over for Section B on *Page four***

*Marks*

**Section B**

Marie-Claire nous a parlé de ses vacances passées à la Martinique et de ce qu'il y a à faire pour les touristes et les jeunes qui y habitent.  Où préférez–vous passer les vacances?  Et pourquoi?  Qu'est-ce qu'il y a chez vous pour les touristes et pour les jeunes qui y habitent?

Ecrivez 120—150 mots en français pour exprimer vos idées.    **10**

**(30)**

**USE THE 4 PAGE LINED ANSWER SHEET FOR YOUR ANSWER TO SECTION B**

*[END OF QUESTION PAPER]*

[BLANK PAGE]

# X059/12/01

NATIONAL
QUALIFICATIONS
2014

WEDNESDAY, 14 MAY
1.00 PM – 2.40 PM

FRENCH
HIGHER
Reading and
Directed Writing

45 marks are allocated to this paper.  The value attached to each question is shown after each question.

You should spend approximately one hour on Section I and 40 minutes on Section II.

You may use a French dictionary.

## SECTION 1 – READING

Read the whole article carefully and then answer **in English** the questions which follow it.

This article describes the increasing problem that Paris has, like all big cities in Europe, with pickpockets.

### Alerte aux pickpockets!

Paris, ville romantique, ville historique où il y a toujours des milliers de touristes. En été on vient à Paris pour flâner le long des
5 boulevards, voir les monuments historiques et goûter la cuisine, connue dans le monde entier. Mais il faut se déplacer parce que Paris est une ville énorme. La plupart des
10 touristes font comme les Parisiens et prennent le métro. Pour eux, l'expérience typique est de se trouver coincé contre les autres voyageurs avec peu de place pour se bouger.

15 Mais il y a un phénomène qui arrive de plus en plus dans le métro. Sur le quai on voit une bande de quatre jeunes filles en jean dont la plus âgée a peut-être quinze ans. Il
20 est évident que c'est elle qui mène le groupe. On le sait parce que quand elle parle les autres l'écoutent. Ce sont des adolescentes ordinaires en apparence mais elles observent
25 attentivement les voyageurs. Quand le train arrive les gens se pressent devant les portes des wagons, et c'est toujours la même stratégie. Une des ados reste sur le quai et surveille
30 pendant que les autres se mêlent aux touristes. Elles doivent faire vite: elles n'ont que dix ou quinze secondes pour plonger leurs mains fines et manucurées dans les sacs pendant que
35 les passagers grimpent dans le wagon.

### Quand on décide d'agir . . .

En général les délinquants profitent de la passivité des témoins. Mais quelquefois ceux-ci décident
40 d'agir. Par exemple, vendredi dernier, au centre de Paris, une petite bande de jeunes demandait de la nourriture. Ils tournaient autour des pique-niqueurs dans le Jardin du Luxembourg tout en répétant 45 «Donnez-moi des chips» «Donnez-moi du pain». Ils faisaient semblant de mendier mais ce n'était que pour distraire les touristes pendant qu'ils volaient un portefeuille, un 50 portable ou un sac. Francis, un policier à la retraite, observait ce qui se passait et il s'est jetté sur un des voleurs, en hurlant: «Attention, pickpockets!» Il a saisi deux voleurs 55 mais les autres ont réussi à s'enfuir.

### Ça peut devenir dangereux.

Il paraît que ces bandes de jeunes volent jusqu'à 40 000 euros en deux semaines. Mais c'est toujours 60 la même histoire. Quand on les interroge, ils promettent de changer leurs habitudes. Mais ce sont toujours les mêmes qui, dix minutes plus tard, menacent des photographes 65 parce qu'ils sont mécontents qu'on les prenne en photo. Mais on peut être menacé partout à Paris. Même près de la Tour Eiffel avec ses 7 millions de visiteurs par an il y a des 70 groupes de garçons qui demandent aux touristes de signer une pétition et de faire un don à une association humanitaire. Si on refuse, on court le risque d'être poursuivi. Plus tard 75 on se rend compte que le portefeuille n'est plus dans la poche.

### «Que faire pour résoudre le problème?»

Selon les autorités il faut continuer 80 à identifier et arrêter ces groupes. Il faut aussi informer les touristes à rester vigilants en ce qui concerne les sacs et les portefeuilles. Ils mettent

85 des affiches partout pour avertir le public du danger. On les voit dans le métro, près des monuments historiques, dans les gares. Mais c'est difficile. Quand on est en vacances, 90 il fait chaud, on parle de ce qu'on va faire, ce qu'on va voir, on ne fait pas toujours attention.

Un policier qui a beaucoup d'expérience avec ces groupes dit: «Ils ne vont pas à l'école, donc ils ne savent 95 ni lire ni écrire. Mendier et voler, c'est leur seul moyen de survivre.»

## Questions

*Marks*

1. Paris is very busy in the summer. (lines 1–35)

   (a) Give **two** reasons why tourists come to Paris in the summer. 2

   (b) What is a typical experience for tourists in the métro? 1

   (c) The article describes how a group of young female pickpockets operates. What strategies do these girls use to pickpocket in the métro? 3

2. Sometimes witnesses decide to take action against the pickpockets. (lines 36–56)

   (a) What were the group of young people pretending to do in the Jardin du Luxembourg? 1

   (b) What were they really doing? 1

   (c) What action did Francis, a retired police officer, take? 2

3. Pick-pocketing has become a dangerous and widespread problem in Paris. (lines 57–77)

   (a) What statistics are used to show the extent of the problem? 1

   (b) Why do the young people mentioned threaten photographers? 1

   (c) The article describes how tourists can be tricked at the Eiffel Tower. Give details. 3

4. The authorities are taking steps to resolve this problem. (lines 78–97)

   (a) What are they doing? 3

   (b) According to an experienced police officer what leads young people to steal? 2

   **(20)**

5. Translate into English:

   «Mais il y a un phénomène …… l'écoutent.» (lines 15–22) **10**

   **(30)**

   **[Turn over for SECTION II on *Page four***

## SECTION II—DIRECTED WRITING

*Marks*

You spent two weeks in the summer at your exchange partner's house in the south of France.

On your return from the visit, you have been asked to write an account of your experiences **in French** for inclusion in the foreign language section of your school/college website.

**You must include** the following information and **you should try to add** other relevant details:

- how you travelled **and** what you did on the journey

- what you thought of the house **and** the area where it was situated

- how you normally spent your time during the day with your French exchange partner

- what you liked/disliked about the French way of life

- how you benefited from your stay

- whether or not you would recommend the area to tourists.

**Your report should be 150-180 words in length.**

**Marks will be deducted for any area of information that is omitted.**        (15)

[*END OF QUESTION PAPER*]

# X059/12/12

| NATIONAL QUALIFICATIONS 2014 | WEDNESDAY, 14 MAY 3.00 PM – 4.00 PM | FRENCH HIGHER Listening Transcript |
| --- | --- | --- |

**This paper must not be seen by any candidate.**

The material overleaf is provided for use in an emergency only (eg the recording or equipment proving faulty) or where permission has been given in advance by SQA for the material to be read to candidates with additional support needs.   The material must be read exactly as printed.

French Transcript—Higher

---

**Instructions to reader(s):**

The dialogue below should be read in approximately 4 minutes. On completion of the first reading, pause for two minutes, then read the dialogue a second time.

Where special arrangements have been agreed in advance to allow the reading of the material, those sections marked **(f)** should be read by a female speaker and those marked **(m)** by a male.

**Candidates have two minutes to study the questions before the transcript is read.**

---

*Natalie, a French medical student working in Scotland, shares her thoughts about the importance of healthy living.*

**(m)** **Natalie, pourquoi avez-vous choisi de venir travailler ici en Ecosse?**

**(f)** J'ai choisi de venir en Ecosse parce que ma grand-mère est d'origine écossaise. En plus, je voulais faire un stage dans un pays anglophone pour améliorer ma connaissance de la langue.

**(m)** **Qu'est-ce que vous faites exactement pendant la semaine?**

**(f)** Je travaille à l'hôpital trois jours par semaine et les deux autres jours je poursuis mes études à l'université. Le travail est très fatigant, parce que normalement je commence le matin à sept heures et parfois je ne finis pas avant onze heures du soir.

**(m)** **Quelles sortes de problèmes est-ce que vous rencontrez à l hôpital?**

**(f)** Je rencontre probablement les mêmes problèmes ici qu'on rencontre dans les hôpitaux partout en Europe. Par exemple, il y a beaucoup de maladies qui sont liées à la drogue et à l'alcool.

**(m)** **A votre avis, quelles différences y a-t-il entre le mode de vie écossais et le mode de vie français?**

**(f)** Pour moi, la plus grande différence est que les Ecossais mangent assez mal par rapport aux Français. En particulier, je pense qu' ils consomment trop de matières grasses et trop de sucreries. Voilà pourquoi on voit des gens à l'hôpital qui ont des maladies cardiaques, et des gens qui sont obèses.

**(m)** **Et à votre avis, qu'est-ce qu'on peut faire pour prévenir ces genres de maladies?**

**(f)** A mon avis, il faut essayer de manger sain—c'est-à-dire qu'il faut manger cinq portions de fruits et de légumes par jour. En plus, on ne doit pas boire autant d'alcool. Et à mon avis il est très important d'essayer d'arrêter de fumer!

**(m)** **Vous croyez aussi qu'il est important de faire un peu d'exercice?**

**(f)** Oh oui, à mon avis, l'exercice est très important pour se tenir en forme. On doit faire au moins une demi-heure d'exercice tous les jours pour rester en bonne santé. Mais, en France il est plus facile de faire de l'exercice parce qu' avec le beau temps on est dehors plus souvent.

**(m)** **Pourquoi vous pensez qu'il y a tant de gens qui ne font pas d'exercice?**

**(f)** Après une longue journée de travail, on est souvent fatigué et on veut tout simplement s'installer dans un fauteuil devant la télé ou devant l'ordinateur tout en grignotant et en buvant un verre.

**(m)** **Alors, comment est-ce qu'on peut persuader les gens de faire un peu d'exercice?**

**(f)** Je pense qu'il y a toujours des possibilités de faire de l'exercice au cours de la journée de travail. Par exemple, on pourrait monter par l'escalier au lieu de prendre l'ascenseur, ou bien faire une petite promenade dans le parc à l'heure du déjeuner. Et finalement, tout le monde a le droit à un peu de temps pour se détendre, mais il ne faut pas exagérer! Après tout, on ne veut pas avoir une crise cardiaque à l'âge de trente-cinq ans!

*[END OF TRANSCRIPT]*

FOR OFFICIAL USE

| | | | | | |
|---|---|---|---|---|---|
| | | | | | |

| Examiner's Marks | |
|---|---|
| A | |
| B | |

Total Mark

# X059/12/02

NATIONAL
QUALIFICATIONS
2014

WEDNESDAY, 14 MAY
3.00 PM – 4.00 PM

FRENCH
HIGHER
Listening/Writing

**Fill in these boxes and read what is printed below.**

Full name of centre

Town

Forename(s)

Surname

Date of birth

Day    Month    Year    Scottish candidate number    Number of seat

**Do not open this paper until told to do so.**

Answer Section A **in English** and Section B **in French**.

**Section A**

Listen carefully to the recording with a view to answering, **in English**, the questions printed in this answer book. Write your answers **clearly and legibly** in the spaces provided after each question.

**You will have 2 minutes to study the questions before hearing the dialogue for the first time.**

The dialogue will be played **twice**, with an interval of 2 minutes between the two playings.

You may make notes at any time but only in this answer book. **Score out any notes before you hand in the book.**

Move on to Section B when you have completed Section A: you will **not** be told when to do this.

**Section B**

**Do not** write your response in this book: **use the 4 page lined answer sheet**.

You will be told to insert the answer sheet inside this book before handing in your work.

You may consult a French dictionary at any time during **both** sections.

Before leaving the examination room you must give this book to the Invigilator. If you do not, you may lose all the marks for this paper.

*Marks*

## Section A

Natalie, a French medical student working in Scotland, shares her thoughts about the importance of healthy living.

1. Why did Natalie choose to come and work in Scotland?    2

2. (*a*)  What exactly does Natalie do during the week?    2

   (*b*)  Why does she find it tiring?    1

3. What kind of problems does she encounter at the hospital?    1

4. (*a*)  According to Natalie, what is the biggest difference between the French and Scottish ways of life?    1

   (*b*)  What does she think is particularly bad?    1

   (*c*)  What effect does this have on people's health?    1

DO NOT
WRITE
IN THIS
MARGIN

*Marks*

5.  According to Natalie, how can such illnesses be prevented?    **3**

6.  (*a*)  It is also important to exercise to keep fit.  According to Natalie, how often should you exercise?    **1**

    (*b*)  Why is it easier to do this in France?    **1**

7.  (*a*)  After a day's work, what do many people decide to do rather than exercise?    **2**

    (*b*)  Natalie thinks that people can easily fit exercise into a busy day.  What does she suggest?    **2**

    (*c*)  What are Natalie's final comments?    **2**

    **(20)**

**[Turn over for Section B on *Page four***

DO NOT WRITE IN THIS MARGIN

*Marks*

**Section B**

Natalie nous a parlé de l'importance de suivre un régime équilibré et de se tenir en forme.  Et vous, vous pensez qu'il est important de manger sain et de faire de l'exercice?  Vous faites du sport ou vous préférez vous détendre devant la télé ou l'ordinateur?

Ecrivez 120—150 mots en français pour exprimer vos idées.

**10**

**(30)**

**USE THE 4 PAGE LINED ANSWER SHEET FOR YOUR ANSWER TO SECTION B**

*[END OF QUESTION PAPER]*

# Acknowledgements

Permission has been sought from all relevant copyright holders and Hodder Gibson is grateful for the use of the following:
An extract taken from 'Un dur coeur tendre' by Catherine Lamontagne, taken from www.cyberpresse.ca 25 August 2008. Reproduced by permission Le Droit (2011 Reading & Directed Writing pages 2 & 3).

## FRENCH HIGHER READING AND DIRECTED WRITING 2010

### SECTION I–Reading

1. (a) • Because they have been <u>working</u> (all summer)
   • They will never be richer/better off/wealthier/they are rich/wealthy
   **or**
   They have money/cash to burn/blow/spend/use up/they have lots of/more/extra money
   (idea of "extra"/"disposable" money)

   (b) • <u>For the price of/if they have/with</u> a mobile/an internet service/a credit card
   (idea of "if they buy …")
   • Popularity <u>and</u> happiness/pleasure (will be/is guaranteed/assured)
   **or**
   You will become/it will make you popular <u>and</u> happy

   (c) • <u>Give/Offer</u> them a gift(s)/present(s)/video(s)/ music

   (d) • They contribute <u>little/a little/a bit/less</u> to the <u>family</u> expenses/spending/expenditure
   • They can use their money for leisure/hobbies/free time/spare time/activities
   • They think that happiness comes from buying/possessing/owning (more things)

2. (a) • She cannot/wants to travel/have holiday <u>to</u> improve/perfect/study languages
   **or**
   She has to work <u>during the holidays</u>

   (b) • She cannot resist/is tempted to/has to buy what she sees in/when she passes/is in front of <u>shop/shop window</u>
   • She buys things she doesn't need/unnecessary things/articles/items
   • She buys/fills her basket with luxury items or/and products linked to/which enhance her appearance/ beauty products (both required)
   **or** All four items of:
   handbag(s); shoes; perfume; jewellery
   **or**
   Luxury items + 2 examples of the four

   (c) • (Too/So) <u>easy</u> to pay by/with credit <u>card</u>/She just has to take out her credit card/paying by credit card makes it easy

   (d) • She has cut her card(s) up/in two/in half
   • She has spoken to a counsellor/advisor/consultant
   **or**
   She got financial advice

3. (a) • They should do some research/make enquiries/ask for/get information (before buying)
   **or**
   Not jump at/settle for/leap at/accept/take the first offer
   • Negotiate/Haggle to get the best/a better service <u>and</u> the best/a better price

   (b) • (Taking on) monthly payments they cannot afford/pay/have difficulty with/that get you into difficulty/because financial situation could change

   **or**
   Not jump at/settle for/leap at/accept/take the first offer (provided not given as answer to 3(a))

   (c) • Discuss the costs/expenses/rates of the phone
   **or**
   Talk to them about finances
   • Set up/establish rules on how the phone is used/on usage/on utilisation

### Translation into English

4. UNIT 1

| "Notre société nous encourage à acheter sans penser. | "Our society encourages us to buy without thinking. |
|---|---|
| "Notre société | "Our society |
| nous encourage | encourages/is encouraging us |
| à acheter | to buy |
| sans penser. | without thinking/thought. |

UNIT 2

| Autrefois, le travailleur recevait une enveloppe avec son salaire dedans. | In the past, the worker received an envelope with his salary inside. |
|---|---|
| Autrefois, | In the past/the old(en) days/days gone by/other times/Years ago/ Formerly/Once/Before, |
| le travailleur | the/a worker/working man/ person/employee |
| recevait une enveloppe | received/got would/used to/receive/get would have received an/one envelope/pay packet |
| avec son salaire dedans. | with his/his or her salary/wages/pay inside/in it. containing his salary. |

UNIT 3

| Il savait exactement combien il pouvait dépenser. | He knew exactly how much he could spend. |
|---|---|
| Il savait | He knew/would/used to know |
| exactement combien | exactly how much/the exact amount (that) |
| il pouvait dépenser. | he could/was able to/would be able to/had to spend. |

UNIT 4

| On achetait les choses parce qu'on en avait besoin. | One/You bought things because one/you needed them. |
|---|---|
| On achetait les choses | One/You/They/People/ We bought/used to/would buy things |
| parce qu' | because |
| on en avait besoin. | one/you/they/people/we needed/would need/had need of/needed to have them. |

UNIT 5

| Aujourd'hui, l'argent est invisible," dit Anita. | Today, money is invisible," says Anita. |
|---|---|
| Aujourd'hui, | Today/Nowadays/These days |
| l'argent est invisible," | money/the money is invisible/unseen," |
| dit Anita. | says Anita. |

## SECTION II – Directed Writing

All 6 bullet points must be addressed.

2 marks (ie single marks, not pegged ones) will be deducted for each bullet not addressed, up to a maximum of 2 bullets. If 3 or more bullets have not been addressed, the mark will be 0.

After this has been considered, marks are allocated for the essay according to the tables on pages 81–82.

| Category | Mark | Content | Accuracy | Language Resource – Variety, Range, Structures |
|---|---|---|---|---|
| Very Good | 15 | • All bullet points are covered fully, in a balanced way, including a number of complex sentences.<br>• Some candidates may also provide additional information.<br>• A wide range of verbs/verb forms, tenses and constructions is used.<br>• Overall this comes over as a competent, well thought-out account of the event which reads naturally. | • The candidate handles all aspects of grammar and spelling accurately, although the language may contain some minor errors or even one more serious error.<br>• Where the candidate attempts to use language more appropriate to post-Higher, a slightly higher number of inaccuracies need not detract from the overall very good impression. | • The candidate is comfortable with almost all the grammar used and generally uses a different verb or verb form in each sentence.<br>• There is good use of a variety of tenses, adjectives, adverbs and prepositional phrases and, where appropriate, word order.<br>• The candidate uses co-ordinating conjunctions and subordinate clauses throughout the writing.<br>• The language flows well. |
| Good | 12 | • All bullet points are addressed, generally quite fully, and some complex sentences may be included.<br>• The response to one bullet point may be thin, although other bullet points are dealt with in some detail.<br>• The candidate uses a reasonable range of verbs/verb forms and other constructions. | • The candidate generally handles verbs and other parts of speech accurately but simply.<br>• There may be some errors in spelling, adjective endings and, where relevant, case endings.<br>• Use of accents may be less secure.<br>• Where the candidate is attempting to use more complex vocabulary and structures, these may be less successful, although basic structures are used accurately.<br>• There may be minor misuse of dictionary. | • There may be less variety in the verbs used.<br>• Most of the more complex sentences use co-ordinating conjunctions, and there may also be examples of subordinating conjunctions where appropriate.<br>• In one bullet point the language may be more basic than might otherwise be expected at this level.<br>• Overall the writing will be competent, mainly correct, but pedestrian. |
| Satisfactory | 9 | • The candidate uses mainly simple, more basic sentences.<br>• The language is perhaps repetitive and uses a limited range of verbs and fixed phrases not appropriate to this level.<br>• In some examples, one or two bullet points may be less fully addressed.<br>• In some cases, the content may be similar to that of good or very good examples, but with some serious accuracy issues. | • The verbs are generally correct, but basic.<br>• Tenses may be inconsistent, with present tenses being used at times instead of past tenses.<br>• There are quite a few errors in other parts of speech – personal pronouns, gender of nouns, adjective endings, cases, singular/plural confusion – and in the use of accents.<br>• Some prepositions may be inaccurate or omitted, eg I went the town.<br>• While the language may be reasonably accurate in three or four bullet points, in the remaining two control of the language structure may deteriorate significantly.<br>• Overall, there is more correct than incorrect and there is the impression overall that the candidate can handle tenses. | • The candidate copes with the past tense of some verbs.<br>• A limited range of verbs is used to address some of the bullet points.<br>• Candidate relies on a limited range of vocabulary and structures.<br>• When using the perfect tense, the past participle is incorrect or the auxiliary verb is omitted on occasion.<br>• Sentences may be basic and mainly brief.<br>• There is minimal use of adjectives, probably mainly after 'is', eg The boss was helpful.<br>• The candidate has a weak knowledge of plurals.<br>• There may be several spelling errors, eg reversal of vowel combinations. |

| Category | Mark | Content | Accuracy | Language Resource – Variety, Range, Structures |
|---|---|---|---|---|
| Unsatisfactory | 6 | • In some cases the content may be basic.<br>• In other cases there may be little difference in content between Satisfactory and Unsatisfactory.<br>• The language is repetitive, with undue reliance on fixed phrases and a limited range of common basic verbs such as *to be, to have, to play, to watch*.<br>• While the language used to address the more predictable bullet points may be accurate, serious errors occur when the candidate attempts to address the less predictable areas.<br>• The Directed Writing may be presented as a single paragraph. | • Ability to form tenses is inconsistent.<br>• In the use of the perfect tense the auxiliary verb is omitted on a number of occasions.<br>• There may be confusion between the singular and plural form of verbs.<br>• There are errors in many other parts of speech – gender of nouns, cases, singular/plural confusion – and in spelling and, where appropriate, word order.<br>• Several errors are serious, perhaps showing mother tongue interference.<br>• There may be one sentence which is not intelligible to a sympathetic native speaker.<br>• One area may be very weak.<br>• Overall, there is more incorrect than correct. | • The candidate copes mainly only with the predictable language required at the earlier bullet points.<br>• The verbs 'was' and 'went' may also be used correctly.<br>• There is inconsistency in the use of various expressions, especially verbs.<br>• Sentences are more basic.<br>• An English word may appear in the writing or a word may be omitted.<br>• There may be an example of serious dictionary misuse. |
| Poor | 3 | • The content and language may be very basic.<br>• However, in many cases the content may be little different from that expected at Unsatisfactory or even at Satisfactory. | • Many of the verbs are incorrect or even omitted.<br>• There are many errors in other parts of speech – personal pronouns, gender of nouns, adjective endings, cases, singular/plural confusion – and in spelling and word order.<br>• Prepositions are not used correctly.<br>• The language is probably inaccurate throughout the writing.<br>• Some sentences may not be understood by a sympathetic native speaker. | • The candidate cannot cope with more than one or two basic verbs, frequently 'had' and 'was'.<br>• The candidate displays almost no knowledge of past tenses of verbs.<br>• Verbs used more than once may be written differently on each occasion.<br>• The candidate has a very limited vocabulary.<br>• Several English or 'made-up' words may appear in the writing.<br>• There are examples of serious dictionary misuse. |
| Very Poor | 0 | • The content is very basic.<br>**or**<br>• The candidate has not completed at least three of the core bullet points. | • (Virtually) nothing is correct.<br>• Most of the errors are serious.<br>• Very little is intelligible to a sympathetic native speaker | • The candidate copes only with 'have' and 'am'.<br>• Very few words are correctly written in the foreign language.<br>• English words are used.<br>• There may be several examples of mother tongue interference.<br>• There may be several examples of serious dictionary misuse. |

## FRENCH HIGHER LISTENING/WRITING 2010

### SECTION A – Listening

1. • It was the <u>first</u> (time/holiday/year) without her parents/family/alone/with her friends
   **or**
   They had made all the reservations themselves

2. • They were of the same age
   • They were (all) in the same class(es)/in her class(es)

3. • They had saved up (for a year/all year)

4. • They did not (have to) get up/wake up (early) for breakfast **or** as in a hotel
   • They could play/listen to music/chat/gossip/talk/ speak (almost) all night/late at night/into the night/till late/late in the evening **or**
   They could stay up late chatting
   • There was a balcony **and** (a) pool/garden(s)
   • They could cook meals

5. • They spent less/saved money on food
   **or**
   They could cook/prepare (simple) meals or food/eat in/it was self-catering
   **or**
   They did not have to go to restaurants/eat out/ restaurants are expensive

6. (a) • When ordering (food)/With the waitress(es)/ waiter(s)/server(s)/staff in the/a <u>local/nearby</u> café(s)/on the corner **or** <u>that they ate in</u>
      • With a/the boy(s)/(young) man/men (whom they met) at the (night) club/disco

   (b) • They found the girls' (Spanish) <u>accent/ pronunciation</u> amusing/funny/entertaining

7. (a) • You can do <u>what</u> you want/choose <u>what</u> to do, <u>when</u> you want to

   (b) • You feel/It is safe/safer/secure/more secure/It gives security (when they are there)
      **or**
      There are fewer preparations to make/do/You have to prepare less/they do the preparations

8. *Any three from:*
   • He insists that they get/she gets up early
     **or**
     They have/She has to get up early

   • He wants to be busy/active/doing something all the time/always
     **or**
     He wants to do lots of things/activities/He hates doing nothing

   • He takes photos <u>all the time</u>/He is <u>always</u> taking photos
     **or**
     He takes loads/lots of photos
     **or**
     He takes photos of everyone/everything

   • He hates/detests (sitting on/going to) the beach

9. (a) • (A long/big/grand trip) with her parents to Australia
      • (Invited) to her cousin's wedding

   (b) • (She is told) it is (a) marvellous/wonderful/great/ amazing (city)
      • To water-ski (in the bay)/do a bungee jump

### SECTION B – Writing

**Task**

Short essay.

**Assessment Process**

With reference to *Content, Accuracy and Language Resource*, the overall quality of the response will be assessed and allocated a pegged mark.

(See tables on pages 84–85 for details.)

| Category | Mark | Content | Accuracy | Language Resource – Variety, Range, Structures |
|---|---|---|---|---|
| Very Good | 10 | • The topic is covered fully, in a balanced way, including a number of complex sentences.<br>• Some candidates may also provide additional information.<br>• A wide range of verbs/verb forms and constructions is used. There may also be a variety of tenses.<br>• Overall this comes over as a competent, well thought-out response to the task which reads naturally. | • The candidate handles all aspects of grammar and spelling accurately, although the language may contain some minor errors or even one more serious error.<br>• Where the candidate attempts to use language more appropriate to post-Higher, a slightly higher number of inaccuracies need not detract from the overall very good impression. | • The candidate is comfortable with almost all the grammar used and generally uses a different verb or verb form in each sentence.<br>• There is good use of a variety of tenses, adjectives, adverbs and prepositional phrases and, where appropriate, word order.<br>• The candidate uses co-ordinating conjunctions and subordinate clauses throughout the writing.<br>• The language flows well. |
| Good | 8 | • The topic is addressed, generally quite fully, and some complex sentences may be included.<br>• The candidate uses a reasonable range of verbs/verb forms and other constructions. | • The candidate generally handles verbs and other parts of speech accurately but simply.<br>• There may be some errors in spelling, adjective endings and, where relevant, case endings.<br>• Use of accents may be less secure.<br>• Where the candidate is attempting to use more complex vocabulary and structures, these may be less successful, although basic structures are used accurately.<br>• There may be minor misuse of dictionary. | • There may be less variety in the verbs used.<br>• Most of the more complex sentences use co-ordinating conjunctions, and there may also be examples of subordinating conjunctions where appropriate.<br>• At times the language may be more basic than might otherwise be expected at this level.<br>• Overall the writing will be competent, mainly correct, but pedestrian. |
| Satisfactory | 6 | • The candidate uses mainly simple, more basic sentences.<br>• The language is perhaps repetitive and uses a limited range of verbs and fixed phrases not appropriate to this level.<br>• The topic may not be fully addressed.<br>• In some cases, the content may be similar to that of good or very good examples, but with some serious accuracy issues. | • The verbs are generally correct, but basic.<br>• Tenses may be inconsistent.<br>• There are quite a few errors in other parts of speech – personal pronouns, gender of nouns, adjective endings, cases, singular/plural confusion – and in the use of accents.<br>• Some prepositions may be inaccurate or omitted, eg I go the town.<br>• While the language may be reasonably accurate at times, the language structure may deteriorate significantly in places.<br>• Overall, there is more correct than incorrect and there is the impression overall that the candidate can handle tenses. | • The candidate copes with the present tense of most verbs.<br>• A limited range of verbs is used.<br>• Candidate relies on a limited range of vocabulary and structures.<br>• Where the candidate attempts constructions with modal verbs, these are not always successful.<br>• Sentences may be basic and mainly brief.<br>• There is minimal use of adjectives, probably mainly after 'is', eg My friend is reliable.<br>• The candidate has a weak knowledge of plurals.<br>• There may be several spelling errors, eg reversal of vowel combinations. |

| Category | Mark | Content | Accuracy | Language Resource – Variety, Range, Structures |
|---|---|---|---|---|
| Unsatisfactory | 4 | • In some cases the content may be basic.<br>• In other cases there may be little difference in content between Satisfactory and Unsatisfactory.<br>• The language is repetitive, with undue reliance on fixed phrases and a limited range of common basic verbs such as *to be, to have, to play, to watch*.<br>• While the language used to address the more predictable aspects of the task may be accurate, serious errors occur when the candidate attempts to address a less predictable aspect.<br>• The Personal Response may be presented as a single paragraph. | • Ability to form tenses is inconsistent.<br>• In the use of the perfect tense the auxiliary verb is omitted on a number of occasions.<br>• There may be confusion between the singular and plural form of verbs.<br>• There are errors in many other parts of speech – gender of nouns, cases, singular/plural confusion – and in spelling and, where appropriate, word order.<br>• Several errors are serious, perhaps showing mother tongue interference.<br>• There may be one sentence which is not intelligible to a sympathetic native speaker.<br>• Overall, there is more incorrect than correct. | • The candidate copes mainly only with predictable language.<br>• There is inconsistency in the use of various expressions, especially verbs.<br>• Sentences are more basic.<br>• An English word may appear in the writing or a word may be omitted.<br>• There may be an example of serious dictionary misuse. |
| Poor | 2 | • The content and language may be very basic.<br>• However, in many cases the content may be little different from that expected at Unsatisfactory or even at Satisfactory. | • Many of the verbs are incorrect or even omitted.<br>• There are many errors in other parts of speech – personal pronouns, gender of nouns, adjective endings, cases, singular/plural confusion – and in spelling and word order.<br>• Prepositions are not used correctly.<br>• The language is probably inaccurate throughout the writing.<br>• Some sentences may not be understood by a sympathetic native speaker. | • The candidate cannot cope with more than 1 or 2 basic verbs, frequently 'has' and 'is'.<br>• Verbs used more than once may be written differently on each occasion.<br>• The candidate has a very limited vocabulary.<br>• Several English or 'made-up' words may appear in the writing.<br>• There are examples of serious dictionary misuse. |
| Very Poor | 0 | • The content is very basic. | • (Virtually) nothing is correct.<br>• Most of the errors are serious.<br>• Very little is intelligible to a sympathetic native speaker. | • The candidate copes only with 'have' and 'am'.<br>• Very few words are correctly written in the foreign language.<br>• English words are used.<br>• There may be several examples of mother tongue interference.<br>• There may be several examples of serious dictionary misuse. |

## FRENCH HIGHER READING AND DIRECTED WRITING 2011

### SECTION I – Reading

1. (a) • (Easily) lifts/lifted/picks/picked up rock(s)/heavy stone(s)/boulder(s) weighing a hundred kilos
   **or**
   100 kilos of rocks/stones
   • Pulls/pulled/drags/dragged (some) lorries/a lorry/truck(s)

   (b) • He has/He has won/He gets (lots of/the) respect of (the people of/in) Canada/Canadians
   • He is seen as/He has left/leaves the image of a man with/having standards/values/principles

2. (a) • To be/become/becoming/being as strong as/like his father/dad/a strongman like his dad
   • Being (like) a/the superhero(es) in his comic books/cartoons
   **or**
   He read comics/cartoons and wanted to be like a/the superhero(es)

   (b) • They allowed him to take unpaid leave/time off/days off without pay (**not**: a holiday without pay)
   **or**
   (He knew) he (always/still) had a(nother) career if he was not successful (in competitions)/He had a career to return to/to fall back on/could come back to the job

3. (a) • When they are knocked down/fall, they can stay down/on the ground/on the carpet or get up/By choosing to get back up when he is knocked down
   • Despite being injured/hurt/wounded (several times) he (always) gets back up, he has (always) (found the courage to) come back/continue

   (b) • (You have to know how to) get/pass/work through/beyond obstacles/difficulties/good and bad times
   • Hold/hang/cling onto/follow/persevere with/reach for your dream(s)

   (c) • Encourage young people to excel/believe in/surpass/outdo themselves
   • (Let them see that) you can succeed/achieve (big things) while still being an ordinary person/someone who is ordinary
   • Help them/(make them see that) you (only) need to make the right/good choices/decisions and work hard/well/strong

4. (a) • (Lots of) talent **and** not a lot of brains/not very smart/clever/not much of a brain/intelligence/no brains

   (b) • (Others can lift heavy weights, but) he has been determined/motivated enough to be/has become 6 time champion (of Canada)

5. (a) • Spend (lots of/more) time with his family/relatives/close ones/next of kin/his son/Tyles

   (b) • Re-join/return to the police/going back to work for the police/pick up/go back/return to his police uniform

   (c) • To work in the communications and public relations branch
   • Because he has been doing this/something similar for 10 years

**Translation into English**

6. UNIT 1

| «Mon fils a changé ma perception de la vie. | My son has changed my view of life. |
|---|---|
| Mon fils | My son/boy |
| a changé | (has) changed |
| ma perception de la vie. | my view/perception of/on life<br><br>my outlook/perspective on life |

UNIT 2

| Aujourd'hui, je sais qu'il y a des choses plus importantes que | Today, I know that there are more important things than |
|---|---|
| Aujourd'hui, | Today/Nowadays/These days |
| je sais qu' | I know (that) |
| il y a | there are |
| des choses plus importantes que | more important things (in life) than<br><br>(some) things (which are) more important than |

UNIT 3

| d' être toujours le premier dans tout ce qu'on fait | always to be/being first in everything you do |
|---|---|
| d' être toujours | always to be/come/being/coming |
| le premier | (the) first/top/number one/best/in first place |
| dans tout ce qu'on fait | in everything/all (that)/whatever you/we do/one does |

UNIT 4

| A vrai dire, je le savais avant, | To tell the truth, I knew it before, |
|---|---|
| A vrai dire, | Truth be told/It's true to say/To tell (you) the truth/(I can) truly/truthfully (say)/Truth to tell/To be honest |
| je le savais avant, | I knew/did know ((about)it/that/this)before/already |

UNIT 5

| Mais mon fils me l'a fait réaliser pleinement» | But my son made me realise it fully". |
|---|---|
| Mais mon fils | But/However my son/my boy |
| me l'a fait réaliser | (has) made me realise it/that/this |
| pleinement» | fully/completely/clearly |

### SECTION II – Directed Writing

Please see the notes for Higher French 2010 Directed Writing on pages 80–82.

## FRENCH HIGHER LISTENING/WRITING 2011

### SECTION A – Listening

1. (a) • Students (only) take/choose/she takes/chooses the class(es)/subject(s) they are/she is **interested** in/that they like/want (to do).
   She can drop subject(s) she doesn't like.
   She doesn't study science because she has chosen literature
   (Takes/chooses/studies) **interesting** subject(s)

   • Students can leave (the school) (building)/go home <u>if they have no classes/without asking (for permission)</u>.

   (b) *Any two from:*
   • Walk in the forest/Going for (a) walk(s)
   • <u>Hang around/out/dawdle/walk about/stay</u> in the <u>playground/yard/open area/school grounds/ campus</u>
   • <u>Return/Go</u> home (if they live near school/and study)

2. (a) • She's studying literature and she's good at that/it's her strongest/best subject(s) **or**
   She is strong in/good at literature/her subject(s) **or**
   She (always) gets good marks in literature/her subject(s)

   (b) • Repeat/Re-do/Re-start the year/bac/Try again/Re-sit exam next year/Take exam (again) <u>next year</u>
   • Abandon/Stop/Quit/Leave/End/Give up their studies/course/studying (altogether).
   Leave school/education

3. (a) • There are advisers in <u>every</u> school/college/They are in <u>all</u> schools/colleges/<u>Every</u> school/college has advisers
   • You just have/It is easy to make/to ask for/ request/arrange/get an appointment/a meeting/a time to meet up
   Careers advisers are available to make an appointment/ meeting

   (b) • They know you/all about you
   **or**
   They know/have your marks/grades

4. (a) • (Renting/Paying/Buying/Finding) lodging/ accommodation/an apartment/flat/a place to stay (at a reasonable price)
   • (Public) transport

   (b) • Give her <u>300</u> (euros) <u>a/every month</u>
   • Fill her car with/Pay for <u>petrol/fuel</u> (when she comes home)

5. • <u>Drugs</u> can have bad consequences for your <u>health</u>
   <u>Drugs</u> cause <u>bad health</u>

   • <u>Partying</u> (too much)/<u>Parties/Celebrations/Clubbing</u> can make you too <u>tired</u>/affect your <u>work/study</u>

   Drugs and partying <u>can affect your health and make you tired</u> – **2 marks**
   Drugs taken at parties <u>can affect your health and make you tired</u>– **1 mark**

6. *Any two from:*
   • To <u>settle</u> (down)/<u>move to</u> somewhere <u>in France</u>
   • Find a job that she <u>likes to do/enjoys/in the area/field she wants</u>
   • Settle down/Move to/Have a house/Live/<u>in the country/ countryside</u>
   • <u>Enjoy/Appreciate</u> her <u>free time/leisure time</u>

7. (a) • Take a gap/sabbatical year/year out/see/visit other/lots of/different/foreign countries

   (b) • **Money** It will cost (her) more money/a lot of/lots of money/It will be expensive (for her)
   **or**
   • **Debt** She will be in debt/will have debts to pay back/refund/meet.
   She will have debt to pay back

### SECTION B – Writing

Please see the notes for Higher French 2010 Writing on pages 83–85.

## FRENCH HIGHER READING AND DIRECTED WRITING 2012

### SECTION I – Reading

1. (a) • Getting/being/waking up/leaving <u>early</u> to fight/struggle against/avoid/beat the <u>traffic</u>
   • Being crushed/jammed/squashed in the metro/train
   **or**
   Being/stuck with <u>hundreds/lots of/about</u> a hundred people (doing the same thing) in the metro/train

   (b) • <u>Partner/spouse</u> is tired after a similar day/a long day('s work)

   (c) • It was responsible <u>and</u> well paid

2. (a) • (One day) she had had enough/was fed up of <u>promoting soap(s)</u>
   • She wanted to give her life another/different/new/more meaning/direction/sense/purpose/she wanted to do something meaningful with her life

   (b) • It was exactly/just what/the exact job she was looking for
   **or**
   She knew that <u>she</u> could be useful/helpful

   (c) • On their <u>birthday</u>, she can take them/they go to (a) show(s)/the theatre
   • When they are (feeling) <u>sad/gloomy/unhappy</u>, <u>she</u> can bring them smiles/<u>she</u> can make them smile/<u>she</u> can comfort/reassure them

3. (a) • You are/she is (often) confronted by/faced with/you/she witness(es)/see(s) illness/sickness/disease <u>and</u> pain/grief/distress
   **or**
   The children are (often) ill/sick <u>and</u> in pain/grief/distress
   • You are/she/it is giving/providing(the children) hope(s) <u>and</u> (a) dream(s)

   (b) • She took/takes/taking children (who wanted)/children went to see Santa to/in his workshop/to Lapland
   • (A) (little) boy(s), who was crazy/passionate/mad about dolphins, went with her to Florida
   **or**
   (She took) (a) (little) boy(s) to Florida to see/because of the dolphins
   • (She took) (a) (little) girl(s) horse-riding/galloping in Provence <u>with her brother(s) and sister(s)</u>

   (c) • Give(s) them the strength/force/power to fight/combat/tackle their illness
   **or**
   They forget (about) their illness
   • (Help(s) them/give(s) them the strength to) accept their (heavy) treatment(s)

4. (a) • She can devote/dedicate herself/her time to her (two) girls/daughters/children/family <u>and</u> do a job/occupation/work/something/(an) activity(-ies) <u>she loves/is passionate about/fascinates her</u>

   (b) • There can be difficult moments/it provides support <u>for the volunteers/(voluntary) workers</u>

   (c) • Why are you/is she not paid?
   • My/her salary/payment is the child's/children's smile(s)

**Translation into English**

6. UNIT 1

| Donc, chaque mois, elle part avec l'un d'eux | Therefore, each month, she leaves with one of them |
|---|---|
| Donc, | Therefore/So |
| chaque mois, | each/every month |
| elle part | she leaves/goes (away/off) |
| avec l'un d'eux | with one of them<br><br>she takes one of them away with her |

UNIT 2

| pour lui offrir un petit moment de bonheur. | to offer/give him/her/them a little moment of happiness. |
|---|---|
| pour lui offrir | to offer/give him/her/them |
| un petit moment | a/one (little/small) moment |
| de bonheur. | of happiness/joy/pleasure<br><br>to treat them to a little moment of happiness |

UNIT 3

| « Ils ne demandent pas la lune, » nous dit-elle. | "They don't ask (for) the moon/earth," she tells us. |
|---|---|
| « Ils ne demandent pas | "They don't ask/aren't asking (for)/cry(ing) for |
| la lune, » | the moon/earth/world," |
| nous dit-elle. | she tells us/says to us. |

UNIT 4

| « Ils sont réalistes et, en règle générale, | "They are realists/realistic and, as a general rule, |
|---|---|
| « Ils sont réalistes | "They are realistic/realists |
| et, en règle générale, | and, as a (general) rule, |

UNIT 5

| ont les mêmes passions que tous les enfants ! » | (they) have the same passions as all children." |
|---|---|
| ont les mêmes passions | have /share the same passions/enthusiasms |
| que tous les enfants ! » | as all (of/the) children/kids/youngsters/every child!"<br>[addition of "have"/"do"] |

### SECTION II – Directed Writing

Please see the notes for Higher French 2010 Directed Writing on pages 80–82.

## FRENCH HIGHER LISTENING/WRITING 2012

### SECTION A – Listening

1. (a) • She (was able to) improve(d)/perfect(ed)/ make/made progress with/was better at her <u>English</u>/her <u>English</u> improved

   (b) • When you are on your own/alone/do not know anyone she was on her own/she didn't know anyone
   • You <u>have to</u>/she <u>had to</u> <u>talk</u>/<u>speak</u> (English) to people [NB "young people" does not negate the point]
   **or**
   You <u>learn</u>/she <u>learnt</u> by <u>chatting</u>/<u>talking</u>

2. • Seeing/experiencing how <u>Scots</u> people <u>live</u>/(the way of) <u>life</u> in <u>Scotland</u>
   **or**
   What (Scottish) people do in their spare time.

3. (a) • French have 2 main meals/lunch/dinner and dinner/tea
   • Scots eat more often/nibble/snack (almost) all day/all the time

   (b) • In France she eats/ate in the school/canteen/*cantine*/ cafeteria
   • In Scotland she went into town/to a/the shop(s)/down/up the street/she buys/bought something in a/the shop(s)

4. • <u>She could go/got home/leave/left school at 3.30/15.30</u>
   **and**
   instead of 5.00/17.00
   **or**
   which is earlier (than in France)
   • Less/not (as) much/not a lot of homework

5. (a) • She had left (all) her friends (behind/in France)/she missed/didn't have her friends

   (b) • When you don't/as she did not speak the language/English <u>(very) well</u>/her English wasn't <u>(very)</u> <u>good</u>/<u>fluent</u>/she didn't know a lot of English
   • The (Scottish) <u>accent</u> is (sometimes)/can be difficult to understand

6. (a) • The host/exchange <u>family</u>/<u>family</u>/<u>people</u> she lived with
   • (The) people <u>of her age at school</u>/her classmates

   (b) *Any two from:*
   • Joined/was in/took part in/went to <u>all sorts/kinds/types</u> <u>of/a variety of/(lots of) different</u> clubs
   • Played <u>team sports</u>/joined <u>sports teams</u>
   • Joined/sang in a/the <u>choir</u>/<u>chorus</u>

7. (a) • She gained in (self-)confidence (in herself)/became more confident
   • She learned to get by/survive/cope/manage <u>on her</u> <u>own</u>/<u>independently</u>/to rely on/look after <u>herself</u>/do things <u>by herself</u>

   (b) • She was/is <u>glad</u>/<u>happy</u>/<u>pleased</u>/<u>content</u>/it was/is <u>good</u> to get back to her family <u>and</u> her friends/to see her family <u>and</u> friends (again)

### SECTION B – Writing

Please see the notes for Higher French 2010 Writing on pages 83–85.

## FRENCH HIGHER READING AND DIRECTED WRITING 2013

### SECTION I – Reading

1. (a) • <u>During the week</u> people are so busy/have so many responsibilities/work, housework, family/<u>weeks</u>/<u>weekdays</u> are dense and tiring
   • <u>At weekends</u> they need/want a change of air/scene/scenery/atmosphere/to experience precious/special moments/to make the most of them (weekends)

   (b) • Her family was not <u>rich enough to own/buy/afford</u> a home/house
   • She grew up in (a) <u>rented</u>/<u>hired</u> flat/apartment/accommodation

   (c) • It means you have roots/want to put down roots/you belong (somewhere).

2. (a) • The birth of their (first) <u>daughter</u>/<u>girl</u>/<u>child</u>/He/They want(s) <u>daughter</u>/<u>child</u> to escape (the) pollution (of the city)
   • <u>Her husband</u>/He spent his childhood/was brought up/grew up in the country/likes life in the open air/outdoors
   • Could not <u>afford</u> (to buy) a/that flat in <u>Paris.</u>

   (b) • Scared/Concerned/Worried about traffic (jams)/holdups/tailbacks/congestion on <u>Sunday</u> <u>evening(s)</u>/<u>night(s)</u>?
   • Spending/Passing time shopping **and** doing housework/housekeeping/cleaning/chores?

   (c) • You have/find calm/peace (and quiet)/feeling of calmness /being at peace
   • You are far from (the) stress **and/of** daily life/everyday life/routines.

3. (a) • There are no neighbours/no houses next door (so they can make a noise).

   (b) • They can disappear for/spend <u>hours/a long time</u> in the <u>garden</u>
   • Go for (a) <u>big/long</u> bike ride(s)
   • <u>Play</u> in the attic/loft.

   (c) • Join/Meet around/Play <u>board</u>/<u>parlour</u> games.

4. *Any three from:*
   • She was tired of/exhausted/worn out by/with coming and going/all the travelling/all the return trips/all the to-ing and fro-ing
   • <u>Friends</u> <u>only</u> came/come in summer/when they were/are sure of good weather.
   • There was a lot of (major) work to do on/in the house/They don't like/do DIY/odd jobs
   • Children were not coming/didn't (want to) come any more/hoped parents would/wanted parents to leave them at home.

**Translation into English**

**5. UNIT 1**

| Un choix que Michèle et son mari Philippe ne regrettent pas. | A choice that Michèle and her husband, Philippe, do not regret. |
| --- | --- |
| Un choix que | (It's) A/one choice (that /which) |
| Michèle et son mari Philippe | Michèle and her husband, Philippe, |
| ne regrettent pas. | do not/don't regret (making)/aren't regretting.<br>A choice that **is not regretted by** Michèle and her husband, Philippe. |

UNIT 2

| Pour eux, leur maison principale c'est celle de la campagne. | For them, their main home is the one in the country. |
| --- | --- |
| Pour eux, | For/To them, |
| leur maison principale | their main/principal/first home/house |
| c'est celle de la campagne. | is the/this/that one in the country(side).<br>is the country(side) one. |

UNIT 3

| Tous les week-ends la famille part le vendredi soir et rentre le lundi matin. | Every weekend the family leaves on Friday evening and returns on Monday morning. |
| --- | --- |
| Tous les week-ends | Every/each weekend |
| la famille part le vendredi soir | the family leave(s)/depart(s)/go(es) (away) (on) (the) Friday evening/night |
| et rentre le lundi matin. | and return(s)/come(s)/ go(es) back/home (on) (the) Monday morning. |

UNIT 4

| Une fois arrivés à la maison, ils peuvent passer le temps ensemble. | Once they have arrived at the house, they can spend time together. |
| --- | --- |
| Une fois arrivés à la maison, | Once/When/From the time they arrive/have arrived/Upon/On (their) arrival/arriving/<u>Having</u> arrived at the house, |
| ils peuvent passer le temps ensemble. | they can/are able to spend/pass (the )/(their) time together. |

UNIT 5

| IIs ont même trouvé le temps de jardiner et faire la cuisine. | They even found time to garden and do the cooking. |
| --- | --- |
| IIs ont même trouvé le temps | They (have) even found (the)/(some) time |
| de jardiner | to garden/do the garden(ing)/for gardening/<u>work</u> in the garden |
| et faire la cuisine. | and (to) do the cooking/cook/for cooking/to make (the) meals/(the) food. |

## SECTION II – Directed Writing

Please see the notes for Higher French 2010 Directed Writing on pages 80–82

## FRENCH HIGHER LISTENING/WRITING 2013

## SECTION A – Listening

1. *Any one from:*
   - 3000 km. from USA/America.
   **or**
   - (At least) 4 hours (flight/by plane) from USA/America.

2. • He got married (to her mum)
   • He found (a) permanent/secure job/work in a (big) hospital (in suburbs of Paris). (both required)

3. (*a*) • She does not see them often/(very) much/She hardly ever sees them/She sees them infrequently/She only sees them there/then
   • They/Her grandparents spoil/indulge/make a fuss of her.

   (*b*) *Any one from:*
   • Her grandfather is not in good health/does not keep well/has health issues/problems/is too ill.
   **or**
   • Flight/Journey/It is (too) long for her grandfather.

4. *Any two from:*
   • Before it gets/is (too) hot/warm/It isn't (too) hot/warm/It's not as hot/warm
   • She likes walking/strolling/To walk/stroll along/on/the length of the beach
   • There is no-one/nobody about/around/to be seen/to see/So that she can be the only person on the beach./The beach is empty.

5. (*a*) *Any two from:*
   • Her grandparents/They live (quite) far from town/city/They don't live near the town
   • Not much/(a) little/lack of/limited/poor/not good (means of) (public) transport
   • (If she wants to go to the cinema), grandfather has to give her a lift/take her.

   (*b*) • Chatting/Talking/Gossiping/She chats/talks/gossips with her grandparents.

6. (*a*) *Any two from:*
   • Water/Aqua/Nautical sports
   • Boat trips/excursions/outings/rides/Going (out) on a boat
   • (Scuba/Deep-sea) Diving (under water).

   (*b*) • Walk/Hike/Ramble/Go for walk(s)/hike(s)/ramble(s) inland/in the interior/centre (of island)/in the mountains/Go hill-walking.

7. • People/They are (a lot) (more) open/smiling/cheerful
   • (The) (rhythm/pace/way of) life is slow(er)/(more) relaxed/laid-back/less hurried (than in France)
   • **or**
   • People/they aren't always in a hurry/are less rushed (like/than in Paris/France)/people in France are more rushed

8. • Because there is/are (a lot of ) youth unemployment/(a lot of) young people unemployed/(a lot of) unemployment among young people
   • Work is (often) badly/poorly paid and you have to work long hours

9. • Become/Be a doctor like her father
   **or**
   Work with/help/care for/look after ill/sick people in Africa
   • Improving/developing/perfecting her (knowledge of) English by
   **either**
   (spending/having/taking) a gap/sabbatical year/year off.
   **or**
   (spending/having/taking) a year in Australia/USA.

## SECTION B – Writing

Please see the notes for Higher French 2010 Writing on pages 83–85.

## FRENCH HIGHER READING AND DIRECTED WRITING 2014

### SECTION I – Reading

1. (a) *Any two from:*
   - To stroll/wander/amble/walk along /down the boulevards/ avenues/streets
   - (Visit/see) historic/historical monuments
   - Taste/sample/try (world-renowned) cuisine/food/cooking/ dishes

   (b) • (They find themselves /are) stuck/crushed/wedged/jammed/ crammed/squashed/squished/cornered/trapped against/ among/in/with (the) other travellers
       **or**
       • They don't have much room/space to move/have little room/space to move

   (c) • One stays on the platform and watches/surveys/acts as look-out/keeps an eye on things
       • The others mix/mingle with/spread among/blend into the tourists
       • They plunge their (thin and manicured) hands into passengers' bags **plus** as they climb into carriage/train/get on (the carriage/train)

2. (a) • (They were pretending) to beg (for food)/Asking for/ Demanding food/bread and crisps/chips (from picnickers)

   (b) • They were distracting/diverting tourists while/and stealing a wallet/a purse/a mobile/a laptop/a bag

   (c) • He threw himself/rushed at a thief/thieves shouting/ yelling/screaming/howling "Watch out!/Beware!/Be careful!/Pickpockets!"/to alert/warn everyone
       Action **and** what he shouted/purpose of shout
       • He grabbed/caught/seized/took hold of two of the thieves/them

3. (a) • These groups steal/make/get (up to) 40,000 euros in/ every two weeks/a fortnight

   (b) • They are unhappy/annoyed/don't want to have their photograph taken/They are unhappy at people taking photos of them

   (c) • There are groups (of boys) who ask/demand tourists/ Tourists are asked to sign a petition and make a donation/ gift/ give money (to a humanitarian association/ charity)
       • If/When they/you refuse they/you run risk of being/are followed/pursued/chased/hounded
       • Later they realise that their wallet has gone/isn't in pocket

4. (a) • They are continuing to identify and arrest/stop/They are identifying and arresting/stopping these groups
       • They inform/tell/warn the tourists to be vigilant/careful with/aware of/keep an eye on/look after/keep hold of (their) bags/wallets/(personal) belongings
       • They put up posters/displays/adverts/notices everywhere/ in the metro and near/beside/at (historic) monuments and in stations (to warn the public) (of the danger)
       Overall answer must show indication of understanding of purpose of posters

   (b) • They don't/didn't go to/attend/aren't/weren't in school therefore/so/and can't/couldn't read or write/are/were illiterate
       • Begging and stealing/It is their only/sole means/way to survive/of survival/surviving

5. UNIT 1

| Mais il y a un phénomène qui arrive de plus en plus dans le métro | But there is a phenomenon which occurs/happens more and more in the métro |
|---|---|
| Mais il y a un phénomène | But/However there is a/one phenomenon |
| qui arrive | which/that occurs/ happens/appears/ arises/takes place/comes up (which/that is/has been) occurring/happening/ap pearing/arising/ taking place/coming up |
| de plus en plus | more and more (often/frequently) |
| dans le métro | in the métro (station)/ underground (station)/ subway (station) |

UNIT 2

| Sur le quai on voit une bande de quatre jeunes filles en jean | On the platform one/you see(s) a band/group of four girls in jeans |
|---|---|
| Sur le quai | On/At the platform |
| on voit | one/you/we see(s)/can see |
| une bande | a band/group/ gang/ bunch |
| de quatre jeunes filles | of four (young/teenage) girls |
| en jean | in/wearing jeans/denim(s) Note: A group of four girls wearing jeans can be seen on the platform |

UNIT 3

| Dont la plus âgée a peut-être quinze ans. | Of whom the oldest is maybe 15 (years old/of age) |
|---|---|
| Dont la plus âgée | Of whom/which the oldest Where/the oldest Whose oldest (member) The oldest one (of them) being ... With the oldest being |
| a peut-être quinze ans. | is maybe/perhaps may/might/could be 15 (years old/of age) |

UNIT 4

| Il est évident que c'est elle qui mène le groupe. | It's obvious that she's the one who leads the group |
|---|---|
| Il est évident que | It is evident/obvious/ apparent/clear (that) |
| c'est elle | It is she/her/she's the one |
| qui mène le groupe. | who/that leads/is leading the group/is the leader/in charge of the group |

UNIT 5

| On le sait parce que quand elle parle les autres l'écoutent. | You know (it) because when she speaks/talks the others listen to her. |
|---|---|
| On le sait | One knows/You/We know/can tell (it /this/ that) This is known |
| parce que quand elle parle | because/as when she speaks/talks / is speaking / is talking |
| les autres l'écoutent. | the others (all) listen/are listening to her |

## SECTION II – Directed Writing

Please see the notes for Higher French 2010 Directed Writing on pages 80–82

### SECTION A – Listening

1. *Any one from:*
   - (her) grandmother is of Scottish origin/originates/comes/is (originally) from Scotland/from there/the region/is Scottish/has Scottish roots/heritage
   - to do work experience/a training course/study residence in English speaking/anglophone country
   
   **or**
   
   to improve/make better her (knowledge of) language/English

2. (a) • she works three days (per week) at the hospital
      • she spends (the other) two days/the other days/the rest (of the week/time) studying/at university
   
   (b) • she starts at/works from 7am until/to/finishes at 11pm

3. *Any one from:*
   - same/similar (sorts of) problems as (you find) in hospitals everywhere/in Europe
   
   **or**
   
   - illness(es)/sickness(es)/disease(s)/ailment(s) linked to drugs **and** alcohol/people ill/sick because of drugs **and** alcohol

4. (a) • Scots eat badly/worse (compared to French)/Scots have poorer diet/eat (more) unhealthy food/Scottish people don't eat as healthily (as French people)/French eat more healthily (than Scots)
   
   (b) • Scottish people consume/eat/buy/choose too much/many fat/fatty/sweet/sugary things/food
   
   **or**
   
   • Scottish diet has too much fat/sugar
   
   (c) • cardiac/heart/disease/illness/problems/issues
   
   **or**
   
   • obesity/people are/become obese

5. • eat five (portions/pieces) of fruit and veg per day/ eat your 5 a day
   • do not drink as much (alcohol)/drink less (alcohol)/limit your alcohol intake
   • (try to) stop/quit/give up smoking

6. (a) • (at least) half an hour/30 minutes every/per/a day
   
   (b) • good/better /sunny/sunnier weather so people go out more often/spend more time outside/outdoors (in France)

7. (a) • sit (in armchair/on sofa)/relax/crash/put feet up in front of TV/computer
   
   **or**
   
   watch TV **or/and** go on/play at computer
   • nibble food/snack/have a glass / a drink(of wine/beer)
   
   (b) • take/go/ walk up the stairs/staircase instead of/and not (taking) the lift/elevator
   • go for a (small) walk (in the park) at lunchtime/ dinnertime
   
   (c) • everyone has right/needs (some time) to relax/rest
   • don't overdo it/relaxation/don't relax too much
   • one/she does /you/people do not want to have a heart attack/problems/cardiac problems at 35/in one's/her/your/ their thirties /early/young

### SECTION B – Writing

Please see the notes for Higher French 2010 Writing on pages 83–85.